During times of trial when it may seem God is silent, Bruce McDonald's book comes across loud and clear in comforting us in knowing that God is listening and is working in us for His greater purpose. Bruce McDonald's ability to make things clear shines through the clouds like beams of light. His words work like a lighthouse guiding us through storms to reach calmer water in our lives.

Todd MacCulloch
Center, Philadelphia 76ers

In *The Fight of Faith* my friend Bruce McDonald inspires you to always believe in the Lord through all the tough challenges you may encounter. When you are faced with many temporary obstacles, *The Fight of Faith* helps you realize they are just that—temporary. With the Lord as your guide you will overcome all things.

Scott Brooks
Former NBA player
Current NBA Assistant Coach
Denver Nuggets

BELIEVING GOD IN DIFFICULT TIMES

The fight of faith

BRUCE W. MCDONALD

MOODY PUBLISHERS
CHICAGO

Library of Congress Cataloging-in-Publication Data

McDonald, Bruce W.,
The fight of faith : believing God in difficult times / Bruce W. McDonald.
p. cm.
Includes bibliographical references.
ISBN 0-8024-3421-5
1. Faith. I. Title.

BV4637.M375 2004
234'.23—dc22

2004012333

1 3 5 7 9 10 8 6 4 2

Printed in the United States of America

I lovingly and gratefully dedicate this book to my family. I am excited for the occasion of this book just in the fact that I can mention them! To Jeremy and Wendy—and our first grandchild, Presley Ryan, to Joshua and Erin, way over in South Africa, and to my wonderful daughter Jessica: You all have been such gifts from God to me. You have made life really fun. I love you all.

Most especially, I dedicate this book to my precious wife, Bev. It would probably take all the pages of this book just to say all the things I'd like to say about her. Honey, I cannot imagine anyone having a better life partner. Thank you for loving me passionately and continually. You have made life fun and fulfilling. Most of what God has desired to teach me I've learned through you. I look forward to spending the rest of this life with you, and then the rest of eternity—although that will not be enough time! I love you "Doc's".

Contents

Foreword

In *The Fight of Faith,* Bruce McDonald lays it all out on the table and reminds us that the Christian life is not challenging, nor is it difficult—it is impossible. And it is getting more impossible as the return of our Lord nears. How can we be victorious in our daily walk when we encounter so many unexplainable events? Why do we get cancer? Why do children turn away from the faith? Why is terrorism taking center stage in the news? Why can't the people in our churches get along?

In this book, you will not find worn-out answers to these penetrating questions. Bruce McDonald has not parroted the solutions found in other books. He has forcefully reminded us that the Christian life is not a walk in the park—it is not intended to be. We are in a battle for our very souls as we enter the closing days of this age of grace! And the fight is centered at the core of our Christian belief. If we try to *reason* our way through the battles, we will lose our way. This is a fight of *faith!* Our only hope is in Jesus Christ!

I have been in the heat of this battle! When I heard the doctor say, "You have cancer," I couldn't help but wonder why God would allow this to happen to me. But now, ten years later, I can look back and see that God was up to something. For the first time in my adult life, I found myself in a helpless situation. My only option was to trust God. I had heard before that before God could greatly use a man He would have to crush him. I used to pray that I could be the exception to that rule. I have discovered that there are no exceptions.

From his background in the world of sports, Bruce McDonald forces us look at life with the eyes of a warrior. He challenges us to overcome the enemy of our faith. He reminds us that God has a game plan for each one of us and that game plan is found in the Word of God. When we go into the battle clothed in the armor of God we can be victorious.

And here's the best news of all! One day our faith will become sight! We will know even as we are known. We will see clearly what we can now only see dimly! One day the victory will be finally and forever ours. But for now, we are warriors and our faith is being tested! We are in the *fight for faith!*

My faith was strengthened as I read this book. I know yours will be too!

DR. DAVID JEREMIAH

Acknowledgments

First of all, Bill Anderson. Bill is the president and CEO of the Christian Booksellers Association. Thank you, Bill, for having faith in me and giving me the opportunity to first present these truths to your CBA board. Bill and Nan, we love you guys.

Then, where would this book be without Greg Thornton? Greg is the vice president of Publications at Moody Publishers. Greg was in that same CBA board meeting and had the vision of seeing this material in print. Thank you, Greg, for your encouragement along the way, and thank you for taking a risk on a relatively unknown author. I am indebted to you.

Long before the completion of this book, Adora Hill took my scribbled notes and early typings and "cleaned them up" before putting them in manuscript form. Tim and Adora, we treasure your friendship. Thank you so much for your labor of love.

Additionally, I want to express my sincere appreciation and gratitude to Dr. David Jeremiah for taking the time to look at my manuscript and write the foreword for the book. Besides being a prolific author, he is senior pastor at Shadow Mountain Church in El Cajon, California, heads up the radio ministry of Turning Point, and carries the heavy demands of speaking all across the country. His books have greatly influenced my life. He has been an encouragement to me and someone I have counted as a friend for many years. Thank you, David.

Last of all, thank you, Ali Childers, for your special work at Moody Publishers in editing my book. God could not have given me a better partner in bringing this material to print. Your observations, insights, corrections, suggestions, and above all, encouragement, were invaluable. I appreciate all you have done.

To God be the glory!

Psalm 115:1

Introduction: A Heart-Perplexing Question

The call came from a friend several states away. This pastor said he was going to be in my area of the country and wanted to stop by and see me. Todd*, who pastored a large church, was a uniquely gifted man of God. I looked forward to his visit.

Not long after his arrival, he asked if he could talk with me in private. My wife went downstairs to the kitchen to prepare dinner. Todd quickly closed the door, returned to his seat, and began to share what was on his heart.

Things were going relatively well, in spite of the usual challenges of pastoring a large church with multiple staff. His family life was good, and he was still feeling the "rush" of preaching a sermon each Sunday. But then he began to share some stories from his ministry to individuals. He told me about a teenager in his church who was from a godly family. This teen

*Many names in stories have been changed.

had chosen to rebel, and despite efforts by Todd and the staff, he continued to pursue a lifestyle contrary to the Word of God.

Next, Todd told me about a couple who were leaders in the church (I believe the husband was a deacon). They started to have marital problems, and in spite of counseling and much intercessory prayer, their marriage fell apart, resulting in separation. Todd went on to share a few more experiences along the same lines. He then unburdened his heart, saying he was beginning to lose confidence in God. "Where was God during all this?" he questioned. What about the stories he had been taught about God's miraculous intervention and provision? Something had died within Todd, and he didn't know if he could trust God anymore.

My heart ached for this young man. What do you say to someone like this? He certainly knew as much (and probably more) theology as I did. It was a very important moment in his life. Though he was not able to express it this way, he was about ready to throw out his confidence in God.

Todd is not alone. Countless hundreds, and even thousands, are where he was that day. The tragic side of it all is that most do not realize that they are struggling. They trusted God for something, believing He would come through, but He didn't. Each time that has happened in such a person's life, something dies. What dies, you may ask? Confidence in God. It may be confidence in God's ability or it may be confidence in His concern. When this happens, most people don't go public with it. Perhaps they are embarrassed, so they continue trying to present an image of unshakeable faith. Or perhaps a person is worried about upholding God's reputation, not wanting Him to look bad in front of others. Whatever the reason for not being honest about our struggle of faith, it damages our trust in God.

I believe that there are many people, even church leaders, who hesitate to trust God for anything new or big because they don't think He will come through. I realize that these are pretty strong words and ones we are a little uncomfortable hearing. But it is essential that we bring these struggles out in the open and into the light. As you will see later, in chapter 5, Todd's story has a happy ending, at least at this writing. But there are so many others who are still in the midst of this battle.

Todd's struggles, though serious to him, perhaps do not compare to those of others. Two months ago, I received a letter from a man who leads a wonderful Christian ministry. He and his dear wife had recently lost their teenage daughter in an automobile accident. He wrote, "Life is not as much fun anymore without Julie. We miss her so very much, and we continue to be stunned by this event in our lives. All we ever wanted to do was be good parents and serve God, and when something like this happens to such a good young person as Julie, it shakes your world to its foundations. It's an unbearable grief and an unfathomable loss that time will never take away." He later wrote a second note to me, including these words: "It's just unbelievable that God would take her from us. We're trying to cling to Him, but it's not easy."

It is hard for me even to write those words from my dear friend. The magnitude and scope of their sorrow is beyond comprehension. Certainly others like him have gone through severe trials—a loss of a loved one, a terminal illness, a financial reversal, a loss of resources, or a failed relationship. Maybe it's praying for years for a wayward child, or that God would provide a spouse or a new job. Perhaps it is relief from migraine headaches or bills that can't ever seem to be paid. The haunting, and sometimes hammering, question is: Where is God? Why doesn't He answer?

This is not a new dilemma or problem. People have always struggled with the "seeming" slowness or silence of God. Here are some biblical examples:

DAVID: *Why, O LORD, do you stand far off? Why do you hide yourself in times of trouble?* (Psalm 10:1)

JOB: *I cry out to you, O God, but you do not answer; I stand up, but you merely look at me.* (Job 30:20)

JEREMIAH: *Even when I call out or cry for help, he shuts out my prayer. He has barred my way with blocks of stone; he has made my paths crooked.* (Lamentations 3:8–9)

The New Testament also highlights these ongoing struggles. The writer of Hebrews strove to encourage Christians who were wondering where God was and what He was doing, saying, "Do not throw away your confidence; it will be richly rewarded" (10:35). These believers who wavered in their confidence and trust in God were facing severe times and about to abandon their faith in God.

Perhaps the notion of faith being abandoned is troubling to you. When I use that phrase, I am not referring to saving faith. These believers, like all believers, could never lose their salvation. They had passed from death to life and had been sealed by the Holy Spirit. They could not lose their faith in the sense of their salvation. But they could lose their faith in God in the sense of their confidence in God. This can happen to each of us, with potentially devastating results.

Will Faith Become More Difficult as the Return of Christ Draws Near?

The intention of this book is not only to remind us of the age-old challenge of a walk of faith, but also to present to you the reality of the increased difficulty of trusting God in these present days. The Lord Jesus prepared us for these increased challenges by His parable and teaching in Luke 18:1–8. This is the familiar parable about the persistent widow. Jesus said He gave it to teach the importance of continuing in prayer and not giving up. This parable can lead us to ask some intriguing questions. It seems as if the widow represents us, and the judge represents God. If the judge represents God, then some very unflattering remarks are made about God! Obviously God is not unjust, cruel, or indifferent. But I want us to consider the last verse that is included in the story.

After giving the parable, Jesus explained it. But at the conclusion of it, He added these words: "However, when the Son of Man comes, will he find faith on the earth?" At first glance, this verse does not seem to go with the rest of the passage or relate to the parable. But it does, and it is one of the most important verses for us to understand in these days. In essence, Jesus asked, "When I, the Son of Man, return, will I find such faith on the earth that will trust Me even when God seems to be indifferent or uncaring?" During these days before Jesus returns, our faith will increasingly be stretched.

I do not believe Jesus was asking if He would find anyone saved on earth when He returns. That would not make sense contextually. It does seem clear, however, that He is talking about a certain type of faith that trusts Him when, from a worldly perspective, it seems to make sense to *not* trust Him. Other passages of Scripture may allude to this truth as well: "Many will turn away from me" (Matthew 24:10 NLT), and "the Spirit clearly says that in later times some will abandon the faith" (1 Timothy 4:1). Knowing the principle that there will be an increase in the experience of the silence and slowness of God will help us prepare to "fight the good fight of faith" (1 Timothy 6:12).

This book is written to encourage you to "not grow weary and lose heart" (Hebrews 12:3). There is hope out there, and there are rewards waiting for you. Your trust in God can have "cosmic significance." May this book be used in each of our lives to help develop us into a people who will have *that kind of faith* for the Son of Man to find upon His return to earth.

chapter one

Where Is God?

We look for light, but all is darkness; for brightness, but we walk in deep shadows. Like the blind we grope along the wall, feeling our way like men without eyes. At midday we stumble as if it were twilight; among the strong, we are like the dead. (Isaiah 59:9–10)

Who Would Dare Ask Such a Question?

In the 1960s movie *Cool Hand Luke,* Paul Newman plays the part of prisoner Lucas Jackson. Twice during the film we are exposed to Luke's struggle with the person and reality of God. In an early scene, Luke stands out in the rain looking up at the sky and says, "Hey, Old Timer, let me know You are up there. Do something—love me, hate me, kill me, anything." He then shakes his head in amusement, and perhaps despair, continuing, "Just standing in the rain, talking to myself." At the end of the movie when Luke is escaping the prison guards, some of whom are really bad people, he hides in an abandoned church. Once again, he looks heavenward at the rafters and asks, "Anybody here? Old Man, are You home tonight? You got things fixed so I can never win." After some more dialogue he says, "All right, I'm on my knees asking." There is dead silence as he looks upward. "Yeah, that's what I thought . . . that's Your answer, Old Man. I guess You're a hard case too."

Perhaps just reading those words causes you to cringe. But don't get hung up on the way he talks to God. Maybe you would never talk that way, but is there something in his despair that you can identify with? Have you looked toward heaven and wondered if anybody was listening? Have you asked for God just to do something, say something, or show some sign? Evidently C. S. Lewis had a similar experience:

> Meanwhile, where is God? This is one of the most disquieting symptoms. . . . Go to Him when your need is desperate, when all other help is vain, and what do you find? A door slammed in your face, and a sound of bolting and double bolting on the inside. After that, silence. You may as well turn away. The longer you wait, the more emphatic the silence will become. There are no lights in the windows. It might be an empty house. Was it ever inhabited?[1]

The Advantage of Not Seeing and Hearing

There is a small branch of Christianity that claims to actually see and hear God. It is not my desire to question the authenticity of this, since the truth remains that the majority of Christians would not attest to seeing God or hearing His actual voice. As Scripture emphasizes, "We live by faith, not by sight" (2 Corinthians 5:7). We may wish it were different. Indeed, we may think that if we saw and heard God we would have our questions answered and our faith strengthened. But Scripture seems to teach the opposite. Jesus said, "Blessed are those who have not seen and yet have believed" (John 20:29). Peter also talks about not seeing and yet having faith: "Though you have not seen him, you love him; and even though you do not see him now, you believe in him and are filled with an inexpressible and glorious joy" (1 Peter 1:8).

As was mentioned in the introduction, it seems that in these days our faith is being stretched more than ever. However, the absence of outward signs and verification need not surprise us. "Hope that is seen is no hope at all. Who hopes for what he already has?" (Romans 8:24). The testing of faith is part of the Christian life. As we see when we look back through the centuries, the saints of God have always been called on to trust Him through some difficult and frightening times. Yet I believe that in many ways we are seeing the seeming absence or slowness of God in greater ways than any time in the past. Praise God that there are still wonderful stories of His moving and His power. But there seem to be many more stories (told and untold) of those who pray and trust for years without seeing an answer.

With every story of a mega-church's success, there are hundreds of stories about smaller churches' struggles. For every testimony of a Christian family's firing on all cylinders where each member is living for God, there are thousands that are fragmented. For every success story about a start-up ministry, there are dozens of failed and aborted attempts. The list could go on and on. What is happening here? Is God partial or showing favoritism?

Confusing Counsel

Rick is a professional basketball player and a dear friend of mine. Rick loves the Lord and has recently seen his wife come to know Christ. He has been diagnosed with a serious nerve disorder of the foot, and the prognosis for his recovery is not good. Not only is there a possibility that he may not play again, but also his walking may eventually be affected. We have prayed and wept with Rick and his wife. He's had a sterling testimony for Christ in the NBA and in front of the public eye. Why are his prayers not being answered? To compound the stretching of his faith, a minister and some of the elders of his church came, uninvited, to his hotel room to anoint him with oil and pray over him saying that God had told them He would heal Rick. (God had not told Rick this.) After anointing him with oil and laying hands on him, they told him he was healed and said to him, "Now get up and run down the hallway." Rick could not, as nothing had changed. The men left that night saying that Rick did not have enough faith. Can you imagine the impact that this has had on his life? He wrestles with thoughts like, *What did I do wrong? Why can't I believe God?* If his struggles were hard before, they have dramatically increased now. Why does God choose to heal some and not others? Could it be the value of the trying of our faith? In later chapters, we will continue to look into these questions. But for now, consider Erwin Lutzer's teaching on God's purposes for us:

> *But how can we trust our heavenly Father when it seems so obvious that He does not give us the same care as most earthly fathers? For example, I know that my father would keep me from having cancer if it were within his power to do so; he would keep me from accidents, heartaches, and disappointments if all power were in his hand. But the actions of our heavenly Father are less predictable; He allows the most heartbreaking of circumstances. Does He really love us? The answer is yes; He does love us—even more than an earthly father could. But He has a different agenda. Our earthly father values our comfort; our heavenly Father values our faith. Our earthly father values happiness; our heavenly Father values holiness. Our earthly father values the blessings of time; our heavenly Father values the blessings of eternity. That is why Paul wrote, 'I consider that our present sufferings are not worth comparing with the glory that will be revealed in us.' (Romans 8:18)*[2]

The purpose of this book is not to address or answer the problem of pain. Several authors and books already cover the subject. This book seeks to present the possibility that our faith is being tested and stretched in a greater and more consistent way than ever before, and in presenting that opinion, also seeks to answer the question of *why*. I believe that if we understand the value of our faith and come to an understanding of the times in which we live, we will be prepared for certain tests of our faith. May we be encouraged to lead lives that have the potential for "cosmic significance."

Tough Times Call for Tough Measures

There certainly will be an increase of wickedness and sin before the second coming of Christ (2 Timothy 3:13). Let's go back for a moment to Jesus' words at the conclusion of the parable we examined. "However, when the Son of Man comes, will he find faith on the earth?" (Luke 18:8). Think what this woman experienced—continual refusal and indifference on the part of the judge. As far as receiving help and finding an advocate, all seemed lost. Now, God is certainly not unjust. He is the most just being in the universe. He is not uncaring or indifferent, but He is sympathetic and concerned for us. And here is where the power of this parable comes into play. He may *seem* to be indifferent. What is important—and do not miss this—is that Jesus acknowledges that God may seem not to care or be responsive to our cries and pleas. He gives this woman as an illustration of persistence, still believing that she will get her answer. In fact, our Lord says in verse 7 that He will hear those who cry out to Him day and night. This is intense, continual prayer. Jesus goes on to say, "Will he *keep* putting them off?" (all italics added to Scripture throughout book are mine). This indicates that there was a time, perhaps a long time, during which he was "putting them off." I know that, in God's timetable, He is never late; but for those of us who are earthbound, with limitations, it sure seems like it. We would all agree with the apostle Paul that God's plans are "beyond tracing out" (Romans 11:33–36). In the book of Job, we find Elihu describing the difficulty in trying to figure God out: "How great is God—beyond our understanding!" (Job 36:26).

So Jesus says He will not "keep putting them off." But why does God not answer immediately? Why does He not seem to be listening or concerned? Nothing is impossible for God. He has the ultimate one-two punch. He is all-powerful (so He's able) and all-loving (therefore He's caring). The answer to that question lies not only in the *timing* of the answer, since He knows *when* is best, but also *what* should take place and *how*.

As we will see shortly, the most valuable thing a believer can demonstrate to God is faith—and not just a casual, passive, comfortable faith, but a strong, vibrant, risk-taking, all-abandonment type of faith. Jesus asks in Luke 18:8 if He will find *that* type of faith, like that of the widow, when He returns.

I have to be honest with you. I want some help with my faith. I often approach God as if He were my servant instead of my master. You know, the old "genie-in-the-lamp" idea that God is here to meet my needs and respond to my agendas. My faith so often seems like anything but the widow's bold faith. Perhaps all of us can benefit by taking a closer look at what genuine faith is. But let me warn you, if you plunge into faith you might get wet!

As I walk to the edge,
I know there is no turning back
Once my feet have left the ledge.
And in the rush, I hear a voice
That's telling me it's time to take the leap of faith.
So here I go.
I'm diving in.
I'm going deep.
In over my head, I want to be
Caught in the rush,
lost in the flow.
In over my head, I want to go.
The river's deep.
The river's wide.
The river's water is alive.
So sink or swim, I'm diving in.

—Steven Curtis Chapman
"Dive," from the *Speechless* album

chapter two

What Is Faith?

The apostles said to the Lord, "Increase our faith!" He replied, "If you have faith as small as a mustard seed, you can say to this mulberry tree, 'Be uprooted and planted in the sea,' and it will obey you." (Luke 17:5–6)

One of my favorite comic page characters is the preacher from the comic strip *Kudzo*. In one scene, he looks up to heaven asking God for a sign. "Please Lord, any sign," he says. Thunder crashes, lightning flashes, and a "NO PARKING" sign suddenly falls from the sky. No kidding, a literal sign that you would see along the roadside. The final scene shows the preacher with a bewildered look on his face.

Desirable Faith

Most Christians have heard and believe that the Christian life is a walk of faith. But just what does that look like? We read about the great patriarch of faith, Abraham, who "against all hope" believed "without weakening in his faith. . . . He did not waver through unbelief regarding the promise of God, but was strengthened in his faith and gave glory to God, being fully persuaded that God had power to do what he had promised" (see Romans 4:18–25).

I don't know about you, but that does not describe my usual walk of faith. In looking at great men and women of faith, we may desire to have a faith like theirs. To have more faith, we observe Bible characters such as Job, a man who lost everything—possessions, children, health, social standing, and the love of his wife. His initial response? We read in Job 1:20–21 that "then he fell to the ground in worship and said: 'Naked I came from my mother's womb, and naked I will depart. The LORD gave and the LORD has taken away; may the name of the LORD be praised.'"

Not only the men and women of Scripture had great faith, but numerous Christians throughout church history also had it, and so do many people today. As I write this, several tragedies are still on the minds and hearts of many, such as the martyrdom of several Christians—the missionaries with New Tribes in Columbia, ABWE's Roni and Charity Bowers in Peru, and New Tribes' Martin Burnham in the Philippines. Testimonies from grieving relatives have been bold statements of faith. For example, Jim Bowers, husband of Roni Bowers, said at the funeral of his wife and daughter, "Most of all I want to thank my God. He's a Sovereign God, I am finding that out more now."[1] Thanking God for his wife and daughter being shot down and killed in an airplane over the Amazon?!?

In 1546, George Wishart was burned at the stake outside Edinburgh Castle in Scotland. Wishart was a contemporary of John Knox, and his death by fire was the match used to light the fires of reformation in Knox's life. Listen to Wishart's words as he is bound to the stake: "Christian brothers and sisters, be not offended at the word of God on account of the tortures you see prepared for me. Love the word, which publishes salvation, and suffer patiently for the gospel's sake. . . . For preaching that gospel I am now to suffer. And I suffer gladly for the redeemer's sake." Shortly after uttering those words, this dialogue took place: "'Sir, I pray you to forgive me,' cried the man who was to light the stake. Wishart kissed him on the cheek and replied, 'Lo, here is a token that I forgive thee; my heart, do your office.'"[2]

It Is the Size of Our God that Matters

We may feel compelled to cry out with the disciples, "Increase our faith!" But notice how Jesus responded to their request. He didn't even commend them for their desire for more faith. Instead, there is a slight rebuke or reprimand. He basically told them to stop asking and that they already had enough faith. It is interesting that on at least two occasions His disciples asked for more faith. One is documented in Matthew 17:20 and follows when Jesus rebuked a demon that was controlling a boy. The disciples did not understand why they could not expel this demon. Jesus said that demons like that could only be driven out by prayer. They would certainly need faith for that. The second is found in Luke 17:5, following Jesus' teaching on being willing to forgive others. The disciples knew how hard it was to continually and completely forgive.

You do not need "large" faith. The size of your faith is not important. You may be thinking something like, *Whoa! Stop here a minute. I thought great faith was desirable. Don't we need large faith? After all, didn't Jesus on numerous occasions chide His disciples for having little faith?* The answer to this question or dilemma is of utmost importance. If the size of our faith matters, we will constantly be focusing on our faith.

I want to address why Jesus would say that the disciples had little faith and then say they did not need "more" faith. Jesus clearly said all they needed was faith the size of a mustard seed. A mustard seed is, needless to say, very tiny, especially when compared to a tree or mountain.

Here is one of the most important, critical truths to understanding faith. Faith does not have to do with size, but with *focus*. Who or what is the object of our faith? It should be God. Having faith in our faith should not be the focus.

Jesus said that if our faith is small but focused on Him, we could move mountains and trees. How did Job, George Wishart, and Jim Bowers display such unshakable faith? *They saw God as their focus*. Their circumstances were so overwhelming that they were not up to the trials they faced. But God was. Because Moses sought and found God, "he persevered because he saw him who is invisible" (Hebrews 11:27). Paul asked God that believers would be assured that He gives them His righteousness and everything needed to grow up in the faith, praying, "May God himself, the God of peace, sanctify you through and through. May your whole spirit, soul and body be kept blameless at the coming of our Lord Jesus Christ. The one who calls you is faithful and he will do it" (1 Thessalonians 5:23–24).

What type of faith is Jesus talking about in Luke 18:8? What does the Son of Man desire to find upon His return? Faith that trusts God in the dark. Faith that looks beyond circumstances, even those that seem to be dealt to us by God, and yet still sees God.

Take a moment to think about the obstacles that Jesus mentioned in His illustration of mustard-seed faith: a mulberry tree and a mountain. The tree is a symbol of immovable deep roots, and the mountain symbolizes seemingly unreachable heights. Jesus says that if you are facing deep-rooted situations, such as those that seem permanent (like generational sins), your faith in the living God can cause them to be uprooted. If you are facing something looming so large that you can't get over it or around it, your faith in the living God can move it. Nothing is impossible with God. W. Ian Thomas writes, "Do not allow the poverty of self-sufficiency to rob you of the miraculous! It is a particularly subtle form of conceit which denies to God the possibility of doing what you consider to be beyond the bounds of your own carnal self-esteem!"[3]

Ouch! That smarts! I must admit that I try to live out my faith by my own efforts and strength. God has a history of putting us in situations that are over our heads. He wants us to trust Him in areas that are impossible for us. I believe that in these last days God is withdrawing a little of Himself so that our faith is stretched in greater ways than ever before. As we will see in later chapters, I believe there is an intentional design to this. But for now, back to the question of *what is faith?*

Where Is Our Focus?

As we have seen, focus is so important. The object of our faith is God Himself. Our whole lives are to be spent focusing on Him who is invisible. "Therefore we do not lose heart. Though outwardly we are wasting away, yet inwardly we are being renewed day by day. For our light and momentary troubles are achieving for us an eternal glory that far outweighs them all. *So we fix our eyes not on what is seen, but on what is unseen.* For what is seen is temporary, but what is unseen is eternal" (2 Corinthians 4:16–18).

How do we see someone who cannot be seen? Through the eyes of faith. Faith is believing more in what we do not see than what we do see. This faith can come from the energizing presence of the Holy Spirit. God's Spirit bears witness with our spirit. It becomes easier to believe than not to believe. Let me say that again. *It becomes easier to believe than not to believe.* How do we handle heartaches, disappointments, sorrow, and confusion? We will, no doubt, feel pain and bewilderment, but God will not let us go. By God's power, we will believe even in the smoldering ruins and even if it is after a time of unbelief.

The clearest and most precise definition of faith is found in Hebrews 11:1: "Now faith is being *sure of* what we hope for and *certain of* what we do not see." This means that when I lose a job, or my health, or a child, that my faith will remain firm because it is focused on and fastened to a living God. "We have this hope as an anchor for the soul, firm and secure" (Hebrews 6:19).

Faith is active and living, and regardless of its size, it focuses on an almighty God. In Scripture we find Jesus talking about the "little faith" or lack of faith of the disciples written about in nine different places (although some of these accounts are repeats by the writers of the four Gospels). We need to understand that Jesus was not talking about the size of their faith. He was talking about the immaturity and incompleteness of their faith. When Peter stepped out of the boat to walk on water toward Jesus, he exhibited pretty big faith, which was certainly larger than that of the other disciples. But when Peter began to sink, the Lord rebuked him (gently, I'm sure) for having "little faith" (Matthew 14:31). I don't know about you, but I cannot think of a greater display of large faith than stepping out of the boat onto the water. But Jesus saw that Peter's faith was still immature because it lacked complete confidence in the One in whom it was placed.

THE RIGHT TYPE OF FAITH

Most of us understand that there is saving faith that is real and other claims to "saving faith" that are not genuine. Not all professors are possessors. Genuine salvation through faith requires putting our faith and trust completely in Christ. For example, there are some who profess that they are saved who have simply made an intellectual decision or perhaps a temporary emotional response that is not a genuine act of belief and faith. They certainly are not trusting in Christ alone for salvation.

Yet among genuine believers, there can be different types of faith. A person who isn't trusting God in all areas of his life is a person of "little faith." The faith that sees the invisible, hears the inaudible, and believes the unthinkable is the type of faith Abraham and Job displayed. Granted, there will be times when our faith is weak. Remember the man in Scripture who came to the disciples with his son who had an evil spirit? When Jesus challenged the father's faith saying, "Everything is possible for him who believes," the father replied, "I do believe; help me overcome my unbelief!" (Mark 9:23–24). Our faith will waver when it is not focused on God alone, but refocusing can restore it. We will see in the next chapter why God goes to such great lengths to mature our faith.

Hudson Taylor's Secret

Hudson Taylor's life has stood as a challenge as well as a blessing to all who have studied it. Like us, he was a man of passions and weaknesses. He struggled on and off, even in his life as a missionary and director of a large mission agency. After years in the ministry, he discovered a secret. I say that because it is often referred to as Hudson Taylor's "spiritual secret." I would encourage you to read *Hudson Taylor's Spiritual Secret,* especially the chapter titled "The Exchanged Life" where you'll find what led Hudson to the realization of "no longer I. . . . Christ liveth in me!" Taylor's story reminds us that "not a striving to have faith or to increase our faith but a looking at the faithful one seems all we need. A resting in the loved one entirely. It does not appear to me as anything new, only formerly misunderstood."[4]

chapter three

More Valuable Than Gold

In this you greatly rejoice, though now for a little while you may have had to suffer grief in all kinds of trials. These have come so that your faith—of greater worth than gold, which perishes even though refined by fire—may be proved genuine and may result in praise, glory and honor, when Jesus Christ is revealed. (1 Peter 1:6–7)

What did you expect when you entered the Christian life? For many of us, we cannot remember because we entered it a long time ago. Some of us, though, remember distinctly that moment when we turned from sin and trusted Christ as Savior. Did we give much thought as to what the Christian life would be like? Perhaps what drew many of us was the joy of knowing and experiencing sins forgiven. The prospects of heaven and a new life right here on earth occupied our hearts and minds.

Soon after this experience, we began to anticipate what was ahead in our walk with Christ. Perhaps we heard or discovered John 10:10: "I have come that they may have life, and have it to the full." Maybe the person who shared the gospel with us told us that if we gave our life to Christ, He would bless us and solve all our problems, giving us verses such as, "In all these things we are more than conquerors through him who loved us" (Romans 8:37). To be sure, these verses are true, but understanding what they actually promise is essential.

When difficulties arise or challenges come, confusion can spread over our souls. Where is God? Why am I experiencing this? When will victory come? Somehow we thought the Christian life would be different. What is God's plan in all of this?

A Surprising Discovery

To attempt to answer these questions, we must understand the place and importance of faith. First, consider what the Bible says about the place of faith. It is essential in the Christian life. We entered by faith: "For it is by grace you have been saved, through *faith*—and this not from yourselves, it is the gift of God" (Ephesians 2:8). We will exit by faith: "I have fought the good fight, I have finished the race, I have kept the *faith*" (2 Timothy 4:7). And in the interim, our whole lives must be lived by faith: "For in the gospel a righteousness from God is revealed, a righteousness that is by faith from first to last, just as it is written: 'The righteous will live by *faith*'" (Romans 1:17). Faith allows us to say with the apostle Paul, "I have been crucified with Christ and I no longer live, but Christ lives in me. The life I live in the body, I live by *faith* in the Son of God, who loved me and gave himself for me" (Galatians 2:20).

We cannot separate the necessity for faith from the Christian life. Colossians 2:6 (NASB) says, "Therefore as you have received Christ Jesus the Lord, so walk in Him." How did we receive Him? By faith. How should we walk? By faith. We are not the only ones surprised by the challenges of walking by faith. The apostle Peter told his audience, "Dear friends, do not be surprised at the painful trial you are suffering, as though something strange were happening to you" (1 Peter 4:12). And to the church in Thessalonica the apostle Paul said he sent Timothy to "encourage you in your faith, so that no one would be unsettled by these trials. You know quite well that we were destined for them" (1 Thessalonians 3:3). We all chafe at the idea of trials being destined to come our way. Why can it be so hard at times? Why doesn't God make it easier? What is it about faith that is so important to God?

Gerald Sittser knows something about the challenges of a walk of faith. In one of the most powerful and influential books I have ever read, *A Grace Disguised,* Gerald recounts the night in the fall of 1991 when an automobile accident took the lives of his wife, daughter, and mother—a tragedy almost beyond comprehension. This man has much to teach us. But as he grapples with trusting God in all of this, he makes these remarks about faith: "I have wondered . . . why faith is so essential. Why did God not make his divine nature more obvious? Why did God not make it easier for us to believe? It seems to me that we know enough to believe but not so much that we are compelled to believe."[1]

I do not think that on this side of glory we will comprehend just how valuable faith is to God. I know it sounds strange to say that something is incredibly important to an almighty God. But faith is. The Bible says it succinctly: "Without faith it is impossible to please God" (Hebrews 11:6). We must never underestimate the high value God places on faith.

Worth Its Weight in Gold

To my knowledge, Scripture teaches that there are five things more valuable than gold. Proverbs 22:1 says to be *highly esteemed* is more valuable than gold. Proverbs 3:13–15 says *godly wisdom* is also more valuable than gold. The third one mentioned is found in Psalm 19:9–10, the *word of God.* The fourth, and most valuable in the universe, is the *blood of Christ* (1 Peter 1:18–19). The fifth, which we are looking at in this book, is our *faith,* especially the testing of our faith (1 Peter 1:7).

While the blood of Christ is of incalculable value, faith is the most pleasing thing that *we* present to Him. Indeed, our highest form of worship is trusting God against all odds. We will not have the option of walking by faith in heaven. We will walk by sight, with perfect knowledge and sinless bodies. But for now, we can exercise faith and trust in God when we sometimes walk about in the dark.

Could it be that God is allowing us to be stretched in a greater way than ever before? Could He be giving us this last chance to worship Him through trust before His blessed Son returns? As we will see in the remaining chapters, there may indeed be an intentional design to our difficulties and God's seeming distance from us. Though we will develop this more in later chapters, it might be good to be reminded of the words spoken in Hebrews 10:35–38: "So do not throw away your confidence; it will be richly rewarded. You need to persevere so that when you have done the will of God, you will receive what he has promised. For in just a very little while, 'He who is coming will come and will not delay. But my righteous one will live by faith.'"

Amazing Faith

Paul told the Ephesians to "find out what pleases the Lord" (5:10). Well, we know that faith pleases God. But are we willing to submit to God and welcome faith-building opportunities? God goes to great lengths to work on our faith. Is it possible to live a life not only pleasing to God but also amazing to Him? Perhaps you are uncomfortable with the idea of our faith being "amazing to God." Is it really possible to amaze a God who is not only omniscient, but also knows our thoughts before we do? (Psalm 139:4). Evidently, it is possible. God has designed it so.

Jesus is the exact representation of God (Hebrews 1:3) and the very image of God (Colossians 1:15). From Jesus' own lips came these words: "Anyone who has seen me has seen the Father" (John 14:9). Was it possible for God the Son to be amazed? Absolutely! Eleven times in the Gospels it is written that Jesus was amazed, and each instance was due to faith. Unfortunately, nine of them were because of lack of faith. But on two occasions Jesus was amazed at great faith.

One example of such faith involved a Canaanite woman in Matthew 15. Jesus had traveled to the region of Tyre and Sidon. A Canaanite woman approached Him about healing her daughter who was suffering from demon possession. Jesus put her off, saying He was sent only to the Jews. After persistence on her part, He then said a seemingly cruel thing. To paraphrase Jesus' words, He said that He shouldn't provide bread for the dogs (those who are not Jewish). The woman still persisted and remarked that even dogs get the scraps under the table. Jesus was amazed at her faith—in fact, He called it "great faith." He then healed her daughter.

The second time Jesus was amazed at someone's faith is recorded in Luke 7. This is the account of the centurion who had a sick servant. He sent some friends to tell Jesus of his servant's illness, requesting healing for this man. Jesus agreed to heal the servant and started for the centurion's home. The centurion responded by sending others, telling Jesus that He did not need to bother coming to his home, but He had only to speak the word and his servant would be healed. Jesus was amazed and commented on the great faith of this centurion.

Why This Faith Is So Pleasing

Both of these accounts reveal much about the type of faith that pleases and amazes God. In the first account, the woman faces Jesus' seemingly indifferent and unkind response. But don't miss this: Jesus is not indifferent or unkind. As in the parable of the persistent widow, He may seem that way from our perspective. I personally believe that Jesus treated the Canaanite woman (called a Greek in Mark 7:26) this way intentionally, to show His disciples and each of us today that pleasing faith goes beyond circumstantial and temporal situations to focus on the invisible God. We see how this woman persisted because she knew what Jesus was really like. He had the compassion to heal, as well as the power.

In the second account, great faith is displayed in spite of distance or lack of the immediate presence of God. This also is a struggle for us today. Where is God? We need Him here. Why is He slow in coming?

Both of these accounts remind us that faith is about *focus*. And focus has to do with *who* God is. Earlier we quoted Hebrews 11:6, which says, "And without faith it is impossible to please God, because anyone who comes to him must believe that he exists and that he rewards those who earnestly seek him." The King James Bible and *New American Standard Bible* translate the phrase "believe that he exists" to "must believe that he is." Pleasing faith believes that God is who He says He is in spite of present circumstances. Does God seem uncaring? Does He seem distant and removed? Great faith (remember, not in size but in focus) trusts Him anyway.

Intimacy Is the Key

It is hard, and often humanly impossible, to have faith in God in overwhelming circumstances. It is easy to lose our confidence in Him. But our faith is strengthened when we believe that He is who He says He is. The way that we believe is through *intimacy* with God. The more we know God (not just know about Him), the more we will trust Him. Perhaps this was the foundation for Paul's unshakable faith. "That is why I am suffering as I am. Yet I am not ashamed, because I know whom I have believed, and am convinced that he is able to guard what I have entrusted to him for that day" (2 Timothy 1:12).

David Jeremiah links worship with trust. He writes, "We worship whom we trust, and we trust whom we know. . . . You must come to know Him before you can really, truly, deeply trust Him."[2] He goes on to illustrate this point by turning to Habakkuk 3:17–19, where the prophet worships and trusts God in spite of circumstances where a fig tree doesn't bud, no grapes are on the vine, olive crops fail, fields produce no food, there are no sheep in the pen, and there are no cattle in the stalls.

What is true for Habakkuk is true for us. If we really know God, we will trust Him. I close this chapter with a look at a story found in John 4, verses 43–54. The events in the story follow the more famous story of the "woman at the well." The setting for this story is rather fascinating. The Samaritans believed Jesus' words, first from the woman at the well and then later from Jesus Himself. What makes it so interesting is that Jesus evidently did not heal or perform a miracle. They just believed His word, coming secondhand as it did. This kind of belief is in sharp contrast to the belief of many Jews, whose belief was often based on signs and wonders. In fact, in the story we will look at, Jesus rebukes the Jews by saying, "Unless you people see miraculous signs and wonders, . . . you will never believe" (John 4:48).

In this story, Jesus travels to Cana where He meets a royal official who has come from Capernaum to beg Jesus to heal his dying son. The official asked Jesus to come to his home to heal the boy. Jesus does something remarkable and miraculous, in accordance with His divine nature. He says, "You may go. Your son will live" (John 4:50). Now, let me ask you a question. If you were the parent in this story, what would you do? This man "took Jesus at his word and departed." Wow! Let's think through what this meant. Capernaum was twenty miles from Cana. This man had no way of knowing if his son had been healed instantly. No cell phones to call home. What would we have done? I'm not sure I would have had this man's faith. "Lord, can't you give some proof my son is healed?" would probably have been my response. But notice something. This man spent the night in Cana before heading home! He took Jesus at His word! Verses 51 and 52 tell us that the official's servants met him on his way home to tell him that the boy was healed, and when he asked when this happened, they said it was "yesterday at the seventh hour." This father then realized that was the hour Jesus said his son would live. Think about it—this man could have rushed home, but he didn't. He believed Jesus. Maybe he did some afternoon shopping while he was in Cana or visited friends in town and told them that Jesus had healed his son. I wonder how he slept that night. Based on the kind of faith he demonstrated, I bet he slept like a baby. Do you have restless nights when you are waiting on God? We can seek to emulate this father's kind of faith. This man trusted God because he knew Him and knew that He's true to His word.

Faith like this is more valuable than gold. Faith like this honors God and becomes a form of worship that supremely pleases and, at times, amazes Him. I believe that we will discover more and more that God is giving us increased opportunities to trust Him as Christ's return approaches.

chapter four

Why Satan Hates Faith

"Simon, Simon, Satan has asked to sift you as wheat. But I have prayed for you, Simon, that your faith may not fail. And when you have turned back, strengthen your brothers." (Luke 22:31–32)

For many years, I worked in the professional sports world serving as chaplain for the Philadelphia 76ers and also conducting "chapels" for hockey, baseball, and football players. I had opportunities to meet many outstanding athletes and count several as close friends. I was most comfortable and familiar with basketball, football, and baseball. When I began working with hockey players, I discovered that they were "a breed apart" from the others. Like most athletes, they are highly skilled and have unparalleled strength and conditioning, but their additional pain tolerance is almost unbelievable.

I was part of a Bible study with several hockey players and their wives. One night a hockey player by the name of Eric Desjardins suffered a serious injury while playing against the Redwings in Detroit. A puck hit his mouth and he lost eight teeth—some of them broken in half! They took him off the ice and pulled his teeth in the locker room.

The next night we had a Bible study with several couples. The Flyers (Eric's team) did not get into Philadelphia until early in the morning. I was not expecting Eric to show up for the study, but in he came, with his temporary teeth and several new stitches. What a warrior! He had been through a battle, and he looked like it. And he shocked no one by going out and playing the very next night.

Lulled Asleep on the Battlefield

It probably comes as no surprise to you to hear about the battles that take place on the ice. But have you ever stopped to think about how much of the Christian life is a battle, particularly as it relates to our walk of faith? Twice in the apostle Paul's first letter to Timothy he admonishes him to fight the good fight of faith (1:18; 6:12). In his second letter to Timothy, Paul says that he, himself, has fought the good fight (4:7). There is definite conflict and battle in the Christian walk. That is probably why the Bible talks about *warfare*. The idea of being a "soldier" is repeated throughout the New Testament. Paul calls Epaphroditus "my brother, fellow worker and fellow soldier" (Philippians 2:25), and he calls Archippus "our fellow soldier" (Philemon 1:2). As Paul exhorted Timothy, we can take Paul's challenge to "endure hardship with [him] like a good soldier of Christ Jesus" (2 Timothy 2:3).

What is this battle, this conflict that we face? Is it for our souls? Can Satan snatch us out of God's hands? No, never! We are secure in Christ. We have passed from death to life and will be presented before the throne of God without fault, without stain or wrinkle, blameless and holy (Jude 24 and Ephesians 5:27). If it is not for our souls, what is this battle for? It is for our faith—not saving faith, but living faith. Satan hates our faith. Let me say that again for emphasis. *Satan hates our faith.* It infuriates him and confounds him. Studies of both the Old and New Testaments reveal countless assaults against the faith of the saints.

We can trace the drawing of the battle lines from what is recorded in the Bible from Genesis 3 on. Satan drew a line in the sand, asking Eve, "Did God really say . . ." The Evil One attacks our trust in God. He especially hates our *confidence* in God. If we study Scripture, we will see a clear picture of Satan's strategy in attacking a Christian's faith in God. Remember when I said that faith is the most pleasing thing to God? Well, the most displeasing thing in the universe to Satan is our faith. He hates it and definitely does not understand it.We are warned in Scripture: "Be self-controlled and alert. Your enemy the devil prowls around like a roaring lion looking for someone to devour. Resist him, standing firm in the faith, because you know that your brothers throughout the world are undergoing the same kind of sufferings" (1 Peter 5:8–9).

We can expect repeated shots at our faith. That is why God's Word admonishes us to "take up the shield of faith, with which you can extinguish all the flaming arrows of the evil one" (Ephesians 6:16). Make no mistake about it—faith is difficult for many reasons, the chief one being that it is the object of Satan's attacks. During these last days before the return of Christ, Satan will intensify his efforts because he knows his time is short. He also will increase his assaults because he knows we will be especially vulnerable during these last days. If God is indeed allowing our faith to be tested in a greater way, then Satan will take advantage of the opportunity.

Satan's Irritant

Let's explore why our faith and trusting in God infuriates Satan so much. We could look at many different accounts of people's faith being tested, but let's look at what is arguably the greatest test of faith. I'm talking about Job. Before we shift our minds into neutral because we are so familiar with the story, let's take a fresh look at the battle that was being waged against Job's faith.

Most of us know the gist of the story. But let's sharpen our understanding of Satan's strategic battle against Job's faith. We recall that Job was a wonderful man. I am impressed with Old Testament saints who lived such good lives prior to the permanent indwelling of the Holy Spirit and the completion of the Word of God. But what's so amazing about Job is not just his reputation, that is, what others *thought* of him, but also his actual character and what God said about him. God said to Satan that Job was "blameless and upright, a man who fears God and shuns evil" (Job 1:8). Now that is quite a statement from God who is *El Roi*—the God who sees. It reminds us that nothing in all creation is hidden from God's sight. "Everything is uncovered and laid bare before the eyes of him to whom we must give account" (Hebrews 4:13).

So if God said this about Job, it must be true! But wait, there is more. God also says Job is unique, for "there is no one on earth like him" (Job 1:8). Now to understand the significance of that statement, we must understand *when* Job lived. Most Bible scholars believe that Job lived during the time of the patriarchs. Space does not permit me to explain and defend this position. But for now, I will build upon the presupposition that this widely held belief is true. This means that Job may have lived during the times of Abraham, Isaac, or Jacob. If this is true, think of the significance of God's statement about Job. There was none like him!

This is a good time to emphasize and remind ourselves that trials, even severe ones, happen to good people, and in Job's case, they happened to a great person. But I want to focus on the conflict, the battle that was taking place here. Since we have the complete book of Job, we are privy to what was going on behind the scenes. We can read the fascinating, yet greatly mysterious, dialogue between Satan and God. The fact that Job was not aware of any of this brings up an interesting question. How much did Job know about Satan? Was he even aware of his existence? What information had been passed down to Job and his contemporaries? The written record of Genesis had not yet been completed. Moses was not yet born. We don't know whether Moses wrote Genesis from direct revelation from God or if the Lord had various people (Adam, Seth, Enoch, Noah, etc.) write records of their times and pass them down through the generations, eventually to be compiled by Moses. But one thing is certain: Job *did not know* that this trial was from Satan (although it was permitted by God).

An Unseen and Unknown Enemy

We must not miss this point. As Job struggled with this fiery test, he thought the cause was either himself or God. Do you identify with this? When you suffer or are stretched in your faith, you may catch yourself wondering what you have done. Or may you look to God and ask, "Why are You angry with me? Why are You distant from me?"

To be sure, there are times when our decisions cause trials and suffering as well as times when God directly allows trials in our lives. But we must always remember that God is not angry with us. He does not treat us as we deserve. "What, then, shall we say in response to this? If God is for us, who can be against us?" (Romans 8:31).

I am not saying that all our trials and difficulties are from Satan. But what I am saying is that Satan will attack us at our point of faith, which he hates. Why does he hate faith so much? Well, let's continue looking at Job. In chapters 1 and 2, Satan fulfilled his role as accuser. Notice the accusations he made about Job to God: "Does Job fear God for nothing?" (Job 1:9). Notice something else. Satan also accused God! Read Job 1:9–11 and 2:4–5. I'll paraphrase Satan's blatant accusation of God: "The only reason Job likes You and lives a blameless life is because You do things for him. You protect him and bless him. If You stop doing that, he will hate You. He will curse You. In fact, God, that is the only reason anybody likes You. You do things for them!" We need to understand how much Satan hates God, and he hates us as well.

When Satan hurled these insults at God (who is patient and sovereign, even though He could've easily blinked Satan out of existence), I can imagine that all of the heavenly realms fell silent. The angels were present, watching the serpent accuse God and probably wondering what God would say and do. God answered with something like this: "Satan, you are wrong about Job, you are wrong about My children, and you are wrong about Me. You are a liar! Job loves Me because of who I am. My children love Me for who I am. You will never understand or comprehend this. But so all of the universe will know both now and forever that I am worthy of all adoration and honor because of who I am, I will let you have Job for a time. You may remove his possessions, family, health, and friends. You will see that he will still love Me and trust Me."

Satan probably smiles and licks his lips. Off he goes to attack Job and, more importantly, Job's trust in God. What follows is recorded in the rest of the book of Job. This has to be the second most infuriating experience for Satan, next to the cross and resurrection of Jesus Christ. He really does believe that Job, or any of us, only loves God because of what He withholds or provides. Satan just doesn't get it!

Cosmic Significance

After experiencing one horrific thing after another, Job fell to the ground in *worship* and said, "Naked I came from my mother's womb, and naked I will depart. The LORD gave and the LORD has taken away; may the name of the LORD be praised" (1:20–21). Can we imagine the "cosmic significance" of Job's act of faith? The whole universe was witness to his proclamation of trust in God. And we must remember that in Job's thinking, Satan was not involved in this. Job never mentioned Satan's name. All Job could look at was his own life and circumstances and to a God in heaven that he knew and loved (remember he did not have the Bible). With hot tears streaming down his marred, scarred face, he looked to heaven and said, "Though he slay me, yet will I hope in him" (13:15). We know God is a God of emotion because the Bible reveals this. We have emotions because He has them, and we were made in His image. I can't help but wonder if God had a lump in His throat when He heard Job say that. Maybe a tear slid down His cheek. I can almost imagine His turning and looking at the angels and saying, "See, I told you Job loved Me. I told you he trusted Me. Though all is against him, and even though I have hidden myself from him, he loves Me." Can we imagine the sound of rejoicing in heaven that day? It must have been deafening. Job had no idea of the cosmic significance of his faith. He thought all was lost and that God was indifferent to his sufferings. If he had only known and could have seen heaven and the throne room.

If we only knew the big picture as well! Satan pummels and hammers at our faith with interrogations like, "Did God really say that?" "Does God really care one iota about you?" and "Why wait on God or trust Him? Take this shortcut I'm offering." Do any of these sound familiar?

Remember Shadrach, Meshach, and Abednego? Listen to their words as they stood before the King of Babylon, King Nebuchadnezzar. He was the most powerful tyrant in the world and held the power of earthly life and death in his hands. He threatened these young men with death by fire because they would not bow down before the statue he set up. "Your threat means nothing to us. If you throw us in the fire, the God we serve can rescue us from the roaring furnace and anything else you might cook up, O King. *But even if he doesn't, it wouldn't make a bit of difference, O King.* We still wouldn't serve your gods or worship the gold statue you set up." (See Daniel 3:16–18.)

God was not only smiling that day, but He was with them in the fiery furnace. They, like Job, trusted God no matter what. They believed in Him because they knew Him. Today, the call is still there: "Will you trust Me?" All of heaven is watching.

Will you trust God against all odds? In these last days, we have opportunity to say yes to faith in God. We can hold onto God and not throw our confidence away.

chapter five

Going Down with God

Now when Daniel learned that the decree had been published, he went home to his upstairs room where the windows opened toward Jerusalem. Three times a day he got down on his knees and prayed, giving thanks to his God, just as he had done before. (Daniel 6:10)

As we have seen, faith has to do with focus. Faith believes God in spite of a lack of visible evidence or affirmation. With this type of faith, God is pleased, even amazed. But believe it or not, there is even a deeper level of faith. It is a faith that not only trusts God *in spite* of circumstances, but also *worships God when He fails to come through.*

I had better rush to put a disclaimer in here. I know God never fails, and when we are in glory we will know this fully. But for now, while we are here on earth, it seems that sometimes He does fail to respond or rescue. Time passes and the answer never comes. It becomes too late for Him to respond. There are many of us reading this who know what I'm talking about. Perhaps we prayed for a teenage son or daughter to impact others for Christ in the local high school, but it never happened. Maybe we prayed for a loved one to find a godly marriage partner, but they didn't or the marriage ended in divorce. Perhaps a long-hoped-for child was born with severe physical needs. The list could go on and on.

Believing God in Spite of the Evidence

Before we look at the kind of faith required when God seems to have completely failed us, let's look at the type of faith we have been talking about in previous chapters—faith that trusts God despite our circumstances. One of the greatest examples of this is the prophet Daniel. I'd like to look at a familiar story from his life from a different angle.

Daniel was a Jewish teenager who was captured and taken to Babylon. The book of Daniel records his amazing life there, serving under at least three kings and two different empires. Though the book contains some amazing prophecies, it is his life story that intrigues us. One such story takes place in Daniel 6. Daniel is now an old man. The Babylonians are no longer in power, and a new king has come on the scene by the name of Darius.

Darius had been conned by some of his leaders into signing a decree that no one could pray to any god, but they must pray to Darius himself. It's pretty flattering to be called a god by one's entourage. But the story reveals that the true reason the leaders did this was to trap Daniel. They hated him and were jealous of his exalted position. They knew Daniel would never stop praying to his God, so they tricked the king into issuing such a decree.

Sure enough, it worked. Daniel was caught praying to God. The penalty? Being thrown into a den of lions. The story continues, describing God's miraculous deliverance of Daniel. But I'm getting ahead of myself. Let's back up and look at what was happening before Daniel knew there would be any deliverance.

When Nothing Is Left

Daniel 6:10 records that Daniel went to his room and prayed *with his windows opened toward Jerusalem.* Now, we may miss something very important. Do we see this fact that his windows were open, facing Jerusalem? Evidently this is an important part of the story. Let me ask a question. Why pray facing Jerusalem? Like many people, we might say, "Because that's where the city of God is. That's where the temple and Holy of Holies are located." You may be thinking of the passage of Scripture in 1 Kings 8 where Solomon, praying to God in front of all the people, repeatedly asked God to hear His people whenever and wherever they were if they would face toward this temple and pray. Here is Solomon's prayer:

> *If they sin against you—and who has never sinned?—you may become angry with them and let their enemies conquer them and take them captive to a foreign land far or near. But in that land of exile, they may turn to you again in repentance and pray, "We have sinned, done evil, and acted wickedly." Then if they turn to you with their whole heart and soul and pray toward the land you gave to their ancestors,* toward *this* city *you have chosen, and* toward *this* Temple *I have built to honor your name, then hear their prayers from heaven where you live.* (1 Kings 8:46–49 NLT)

That was a wonderful prayer by Solomon, and I am sure that in the following years God answered His children's cry for help. However, Daniel's story takes place almost four hundred years later. And guess what! There was no temple and no city—it was gone! It had been destroyed completely. You can read the account of this destruction and dismantling in 2 Kings 25 and 2 Chronicles 36. One verse puts it succinctly: "They set fire to God's temple and broke down the wall of Jerusalem; they burned all the palaces and destroyed everything of value there" (2 Chronicles 36:19). Several years after Daniel's time, Nehemiah inspected the ruins and found he couldn't even approach some of the walls and gates because the rubble was so deep (Nehemiah 2:14).

Now what does all this mean? What does this have to do with faith? Daniel opened his windows toward Jerusalem, several hundred miles from Babylon, when he prayed to God, even though no temple was there. It was gone. God, was defeated! You probably don't like that statement, but think of it from the view of Daniel and his contemporaries. God had lost to the Babylonian gods and armies. The unthinkable had happened. The walls were broken down, the city was burned, and, unbelievably, the temple was destroyed. The Jews thought that would *never* happen. Even when they were wicked and rebellious, in the back of their minds they knew that eventually God would forgive them. They believed that His temple would never fall or be destroyed. And then it happened. Their last line of defense was gone. The unthinkable happened. It was over. The end had come with lost hopes and dreams. It was all gone.

Unshakable Belief

One man and his three friends believed in spite of circumstances. To Daniel, it didn't matter that the city and temple were gone—he still believed God. He trusted God *as if the city and temple were still there.* God's promises would not fail. Somehow, God would do all that He had said He would do. Daniel looked out his windows with the eyes of faith and believed God. He believed God to the extent that he was willing to die. He would still pray to the living and all-powerful God, even if it meant being thrown into a lions' den. Such faith believes God in spite of circumstances. It is faith that pleases God. No wonder God told Daniel "he was highly esteemed" (Daniel 9:23).

But what about faith that trusts God and worships Him when He seems to fail us, and *still* He does not come through as we had hoped? Remember the opening story about Todd? He was the young pastor who came to me, questioning his confidence in God. As he told me about his hurt and confusion, I sat there silently. I could both identify with and appreciate his struggles. He obviously knew all the "right" answers and had undoubtedly shared those answers with others in counseling situations. But as we sat in my office, I knew he needed something beyond scripted answers. It was a crucial moment in this man's life.

The Unthinkable Question

After sitting there quietly for a brief time, I asked him an important question. In fact, if God ever leads us this far in our journey of faith, it is the most important question we will ever deal with. I asked him *if he was ready to go down with God.* The look on his face was probably similar to the look on yours right now. "Down with God? What does that mean? God's not going down." Many of us will face this question in our journeys of faith, though we may try to avoid it. But what if God does not come through? What if it seems as though He has utterly failed us and the time in which He could have intervened has run out? What if God seems to be defeated by circumstances and foes? Are we willing to go down with God?

Do we have a "backup" plan? Is God all we hope for and in? I told Todd that the man whose faith was tested the most had to come to that determination. That man is Job, whose example we have looked at already. Remember what Job said? "Though he slay me, yet will I hope in him" (Job 13:15).What? God slay him? What kind of talk is that? Job was being honest. He didn't know where this attack was coming from. "If God chooses to kill me, I will still trust Him!" What a marvelous proclamation of faith.

Can we get to the point of saying, "All my hope, all my trust is in God. If God doesn't come through, if it all isn't true, I have no backup plan. I will go down with Him. All my weight is cast upon Him." Remember Peter's words? Jesus' followers were confused and offended by what He was saying. Many of them started to leave. Jesus turned to the Twelve and asked them if they wanted to leave too. Peter responded, "Lord, to whom shall we go? You have the words of eternal life. We believe and know that you are the Holy One of God" (John 6:68–69).

Perhaps when we are alone and can hear our most inward thoughts, we've wondered, *Is God really there? Why doesn't He answer? It's too late for Him to come through now. Can I really trust Him?* In that moment we must make a choice as to whether we will go down with God. Will we step off that cliff and be abandoned to Him?

Rick Warren writes, "The fact that earth is not our ultimate home explains why, as followers of Jesus, we experience difficulty, sorrow, and rejection in this world. It also explains why some of God's promises seem unfulfilled, some prayers seem unanswered, and some circumstances seem unfair. This is not the end of the story.

"In order to keep us from becoming too attached to earth, God allows us to feel a significant amount of discontent and dissatisfaction in life—longings that will never be fulfilled on this side of eternity."[1]

Of course God will never really "go down." He is, as the hymn writer penned, "immortal, invisible, God only wise." He will accomplish all He intends to do. But, in this life of faith on planet Earth, it will seem that He is failing at times and that He is even defeated. It is in these moments we must make a choice. Will we go down with Him? It's all or nothing.

chapter six

Help in the Conflict

God is our refuge and strength, an ever-present help in trouble. Therefore we will not fear, though the earth give way and the mountains fall into the heart of the sea, though its waters roar and foam and the mountains quake with their surging. (Psalm 46:1–3)

One of my favorite movies is *The Princess Bride.* It is both an adventure and a sidesplitting comedy. I love the sword-fighting scenes. In one of the scenes, the hero Wesley, masquerading as the "Dread Pirate Roberts," was fighting Inigo Montoya, an unbelievably skilled swordsman. During the battle, the masked man, Wesley, was losing to Montoya. But interestingly, Wesley smiled as he was losing. Montoya asked him why he was smiling. Wesley answered, "Because I know something you don't know."

"And what is that?" Montoya asked.

Wesley answered, "I am not left-handed."

Montoya revealed that he wasn't left-handed either, and the battle continued. Yet Wesley was smiling because of something greater. Regardless of whatever tricks they possessed, Wesley knew that he was the better fighter and that he would win the battle. He could take some setbacks while fighting because he knew this. He easily defeated Montoya to a point that Montoya said to him, "You are marvelous."

We Know Something the Enemy Wishes We Didn't Know

Like Wesley, we may seem to be on the edge of defeat, but we can take confidence in the fact that our victory is inevitable. We'll win! Make no mistake about it. There have been and will continue to be frightening and harrowing times here on earth. We are no match for the Enemy. Victory is assured because we have One on our side who is greater than our foe. And greater is He who is in us than the Evil One who is in the world.

In the hymn "A Mighty Fortress is Our God," Martin Luther wrote: "Did we in our own strength confide, our striving would be losing. Were not the right Man on our side, the Man of God's own choosing. . . . The Prince of Darkness grim—we tremble not for him. His rage we can endure, for lo! his doom is sure. One little word shall fell him."

There probably will not always be a smile on our faces when we are in the thick of battle. But there can be a smile in our hearts. We know something that the Enemy wishes we didn't know. We are not helpless, nor are our situations hopeless, because of who our God is. We can always take strength in these words of Jesus: "This sickness [or any situation] will not end in death [or defeat]. No, it is for God's glory so that God's Son may be glorified through it" (John 11:4).

The fight of faith can and will end in victory for us if we understand God's truth and take hold of what He has given us. Already we have looked at understanding the times in which we live, what faith is, how important our faith is to God, and how much Satan hates our faith. As we dig deeper, we will discover more about what God has provided to strengthen us through our battles of faith.

The Prayer Life of Jesus

A help many of us seldom consider is the prayer life of Jesus. I am not merely talking about His earthly prayer life, though studying it is highly profitable since we know the priority He placed on prayer. Luke highlights its importance in the gospel he recorded. For example, "Jesus often withdrew to lonely places and prayed" (5:16), "One of those days Jesus went out to a mountainside to pray, and spent the night praying to God" (6:12), "As he was praying . . ." (9:29), and "He withdrew about a stone's throw beyond them, knelt down and prayed" (22:41).

How wonderful to have observed His prayer life. The disciples saw it and asked Jesus to teach them how to pray (11:1). But I want us to realize the value and help of Jesus' prayer life today, as He is seated at the right hand of the Father in heaven. Hebrews 7:25 says, "Therefore he is able to save completely those who come to God through him, because *he always lives to intercede for them.*" Jesus has accomplished His work on earth, but He still ministers for us in heaven. He is called our High Priest. "Therefore, since we have a great high priest who has gone through the heavens, Jesus the Son of God, let us hold firmly to the *faith* we profess. For we do not have a high priest who is unable to sympathize with our weaknesses, but we have one who has been tempted in every way, just as we are—yet was without sin. Let us then approach the throne of grace with confidence, so that we may receive mercy and find grace to help us in our time of need" (Hebrews 4:14–16).

Think about it: Jesus prays for us! Could we have anyone better praying for us? Could anyone in the universe be found with more power? Do you know how often God the Father hears and answers Jesus' prayers? One hundred percent of the time! Jesus reminded His followers that the Father always hears when He prays. We read: "Then Jesus looked up and said, 'Father, I thank you that you have heard me. I knew that you always hear me'" (John 11:41–42). God the Father always hears Jesus pray, and God the Father is always pleased with Jesus. "This is my

Son, whom I love; with him I am well pleased" (Matthew 17:5). How wonderful to have the Son praying to the Father on our behalf. We actually have a written account of Jesus praying for us while He was still on earth. In Jesus' High Priestly Prayer found in John 17, He prays for the disciples at length. But then He prays, "My prayer is not for them alone. I pray also for those who will believe in me through their message" (John 17:20). On behalf of His followers, He asked the Father to "protect them by the power of your name—the name you gave me—so that they may be one as we are one" (17:11). Jesus prayed for our protection and unity with the Trinity and other believers, and He still prays for us today.

JESUS PRAYS FOR US INDIVIDUALLY

We can get another glimpse of this during Jesus' earthly ministry. Jesus warned Peter about Satan's desire to attack his faith: "Simon, Simon, Satan has asked [and Satan must always ask God for permission] to sift you as wheat. But *I have prayed for you,* Simon, that your *faith* may not fail" (Luke 22:31–32). Jesus specifically prays for us as it relates to our faith. Through the passage we looked at earlier in Hebrews 4, we know that Jesus, our High Priest, is interceding for the "faith we profess."

Your friends and family members may approach you and ask you to pray for them. Perhaps they respect your prayer life and think you are closer to God than they are. Or maybe they believe that God hears *your* prayers more than theirs. But think about it. The best person to approach for prayer is Jesus, fully God and fully Man. I'm not just talking about praying in Jesus' name, as wonderful as that is. But I'm talking about Jesus actually praying on our behalf, which is a great comfort and help. We can smile, because we know that in difficult situations, our Sovereign Savior is praying that our faith will not fail.

By the way, sometimes we may not personalize the prayer life of Jesus. We may think of it as the "love of God." We may assert, "Sure, God loves us. But isn't it kind of a generic love?"

The answer is no—God's love is not generic. It is personal and passionate. Christ's prayer life for us is not generic either. That is why Scripture points out that Jesus is a sympathetic High Priest. He was tempted in all areas as we are. He not only was tempted, but He also suffered. "Because he himself suffered when he was tempted, he is able to *help* those who are being tempted" (Hebrews 2:18). Jesus enters into our trials and sufferings and prays specifically, personally, and powerfully for us.

Fellow believers also share their struggles with one another, enabling members of God's family to unite in prayer and in seeking His will. Praise God for praying brothers and sisters in Christ! God richly pours out His goodness upon us, as evidenced by the prayers of friends, the Lord Jesus Christ, and, additionally, the mighty Holy Spirit. Romans 8:27 tells us that "the Spirit intercedes for the saints in accordance with God's will." God has clearly not left us to fight the battle of faith alone.

The Importance of Intimacy with God

As I mentioned earlier, for several years my wife and I had the joy and privilege of working with people who were professional athletes. Since we knew many people whose names and faces were found on sports magazine covers and cereal boxes, we were often asked what it was like knowing "so-and-so." You may be able to guess the answer. They are real people, with real needs. It was always a delight to introduce an athlete who was famous (in the world's eyes) to friends and acquaintances. You could tell by looking at our friends how great the moment was for them. Later they would ask us, "What's it like being in their homes or having them in your home?"

I remember one intimate and rather humorous occasion. Former Philadelphia 76er and current TNT sports announcer Charles Barkley and his wife, Maureen, were at our home for dinner. After dinner, we played Scattergories with our three children. The phone rang and our youngest son, age fourteen at the time, answered it. A few minutes later he came back into the living room saying that his friend, Andy, was on his way over. I asked Josh if he had told Andy that Charles was with us. He said no, and I suddenly got an idea. Andy, like thousands of kids, was a Charles Barkley fan. I asked Charles if he would play along with a little trick I wanted to play on Andy. Charles, being the good-natured and encouraging friend he was, said he'd gladly do it. I told him to run to Andy as he came in, shake his hand, and say, "Andy? Andy Jenks? I have always wanted to meet you." When Andy walked in, Charles got up off the floor where we were playing the game, ran to Andy, shook his hand, and said how much he had always wanted to meet him. You can imagine the look on Andy's face! He had met one of his heroes, up close and personal. I'm sure Andy told others how he had met Charles Barkley and, perhaps after time, even stretched it to saying he was a friend of Charles.

NAME-DROPPING: "I KNOW GOD!"

Have you ever thought about anyone famous with whom you would like to be on intimate terms? Well, can you imagine anyone more famous or more important than God!?! We can be on intimate terms with God, and there is nothing like it! The famous of this world quickly lose their luster and attraction. My three children, all grown adults, were with athletes most of their young lives. But after a while, Jeremy, Joshua, and Jessica lost their interest in being in these people's homes or even being at home with us when a famous athlete visited us. But that will never happen with God, or at least it shouldn't. God wants us to draw close to Him. He wants us to spend time with Him. Intimacy with God helps us in our faith walk, because spending time with God allows us to get to know Him, and knowing Him strengthens our confidence in Him.

What is the proudest moment of your life? What have you found yourself repeatedly boasting about (not merely being appreciative of) to yourself or to others? Is it a person—a spouse, parent, or child? Is it a possession—a house, car, collection, or wardrobe? Is it an achievement—your physique, title, degree, or education? What about power—influence, fame, or a position over others? Believe it or not, Scripture says that it is good to boast about something: "This is what the LORD says: 'Let not the wise man boast of his wisdom or the strong man boast of his strength or the rich man boast of his riches, but let him who boasts boast about this: that he understands and *knows* me'" (Jeremiah 9:23–24). None of us likes "name-dropping." In fact, some may be uncomfortable that I wrote about a famous athlete. That's okay. But there is one name we should never be ashamed to "drop." Three times Scripture says, "let him who boasts, boast in the Lord."

Think about it: the God of Glory wants to spend time with us. One of the most intriguing passages of Scripture to me is the account in Luke 24 of Jesus walking on the road to Emmaus. Jesus had just risen from the grave and appeared to two travelers who were discussing the crucifixon. What was He doing there? Why didn't He go to the temple and show Himself? He could have appeared to Herod or Pilate or even the Jewish leaders. Why not spend the day with Peter, James, John, Mary, or Lazarus? Yet He was out on some dusty road conversing with these two and was in no hurry to leave. You know what? I believe Jesus liked their company. He enjoyed intimate conversation and fellowship with them.

One of the most embarrassing elements about being a follower of Christ is that God wants to spend more time with us than we do with Him. Listen to what Jesus says to His disciples: "I am going there to prepare a place for you. And if I go and prepare a place for you, I will come back and *take you to be with me* that you also may be where I am." He then prays: "Father, I want those you have given me to *be with me* where I am" (John 14:2–3; 17:24).

The Godhead desires communion with us, and the more time we spend with God, the greater our confidence is in Him. The apostle Paul's closeness with God gave him the strength to endure through "suffering for the gospel, by the power of God, who has saved us and called us to a holy life—not because of anything we have done but because of his own purpose and grace. . . . I am not ashamed [to suffer], because *I know whom I have believed,* and am convinced that he is able to guard what I have entrusted to him for that day" (2 Timothy 1:8–9, 12). We may be confused about what is happening to us. We may feel hurt or abandoned by God. But even in the midst of those times, we won't throw our confidence in God away. We may not know the *how* or *why* or the current outcome of a situation, but we know *who* is sovereign over all.

Staying in the Tent

Intimacy with and knowledge of our Lord is essential to a strong walk of faith. The great biblical hero Joshua had many wonderful experiences with God. What made him that way? He knew God. He spent time with Him, even before he became a famous leader. Early in his life, he cultivated time with God. A verse that describes Joshua's intimate relationship with God is found in Exodus 33:11: "The LORD would speak to Moses face to face, as a man speaks with his friend. Then Moses would return to the camp, but his young aide Joshua son of Nun *did not leave the tent.*" The tent was where Moses and Joshua went to meet with God. Evidently, Joshua would linger in the presence of the Lord. Our time spent with God will determine how well we respond to trials. We must get to know God, gain confidence in Him, and even boast in the fact that we, by His grace, know Him. As the attacks on our faith increase, we must grow in our intimacy with God.

chapter seven

Knowing the Game Plan

Do your best to present yourself to God as one approved, a workman who does not need to be ashamed and who correctly handles the word of truth. (2 Timothy 2:15)

Sports stars take some pretty strong hits, especially relating to their intelligence or lack of it. An article appeared on the Internet a few years ago entitled "Why Sports Scholarship is an Oxymoron." In the excerpts below, I have omitted the names of the players and coaches to protect them from embarrassment.

"You guys pair up in groups of three, then line up in a circle." (A college football coach)

"You guys line up alphabetically by height." (Another college football coach)

"The ballparks have gotten too crowded. That's why nobody goes to see the games anymore." (A professional baseball coach)

"I'm going to graduate on time, no matter how long it takes." (A college basketball player)

> "Nobody in football should be called a genius. A genius is a guy like Norman Einstein." (A former football player and current sports commentator)

Like I said, athletes take some hard hits, but perhaps none more so than football players. Think they're mentally challenged? You might want to think again. My wife and I once stayed with a friend who is with the NFL. Our friend, an offensive lineman, is 6 feet 3 inches and weighs 335 pounds. During a visit to his home, he showed me a copy of the playbook for Sunday's upcoming game. I was stunned. It was eighty-three pages long! I thumbed through it, wondering how any player could memorize so many plays—those of his team and the opposing team. Our friend told us how important it is to know the coach's instructions as well as the opposing team's plans.

The Christian's Playbook

My friend's playbook was just for one game, on one day. It is hard to imagine memorizing playbooks throughout an entire season. There are preseason games, sixteen regular season games, and, hopefully, playoff games. An athlete must not enter a season or a game unprepared. And what is true for an athlete is doubly true for a Christian. We cannot run out on the field of life without a playbook and expect good outcomes. Our playbook is the Bible. The conflict we face is not just for one day or season. It is for life!

The Word of God is more than a book to develop spiritual disciplines. It is neither a dry and dusty history of the ancient world nor just a large book of doctrine and dogma. It is a source of life for all of us. I have written in the back of my Bible this excerpt taken from George Mueller's diary. It was written so long ago that I'm not sure where to find it again. But what I copied is: "I meditate on the New Testament early in the morning, asking the Lord's blessings upon His Word, searching into every verse, *not for public ministry,* but for food for my own soul."

His diary later reads, "The vigor of our spiritual life will be in proportion to the place held by the Word in our life and thoughts."

We will be anemic Christians if we do not regularly digest the Word of God. Jeremiah used the analogy of feeding on God's promises, saying, "When your words came, I ate them; they were my joy and my heart's delight, for I bear your name, O LORD God Almighty" (15:16). Our faith, that is, our battle of faith, will fail if we are not consistently in the Word of God. As we read in the book of Psalms: "If your law had not been my delight, I would have perished in my affliction. . . . Great peace have they who love your law, and nothing can make them stumble" (119:92, 165). God's Word sustains us and keeps us focused on God during trials. As I mentioned earlier, Satan hates our faith and wants us to look at circumstances and respond to feelings. But the individual who is immersed in the Word sees through that, all the way to God.

In Ephesians 6:17, we find the only piece of the armor of God that is offensive and not defensive, "the sword of the Spirit, which is the word of God." The author of Hebrews describes the Bible this way: "For the word of God is living and active. Sharper than any double-edged sword, it penetrates even to dividing soul and spirit, joints and marrow; it judges the thoughts and attitudes of the heart" (4:12). How powerful is the Word of God! A few of the benefits of taking Scripture to heart are as follows:

Comfort (Psalm 119:28, 50, 52, 76)
Guidance (Psalm 119:35, 105, 133)
Protection (Psalm 119:11, 24)
Rebuke (2 Timothy 3:16)
Correction (2 Timothy 3:16)
Instruction (2 Timothy 3:16)
Purity (Psalm 119:9)
Peace (Psalm 119:165)
Doctrine (2 Timothy 3:16)
Salvation (Romans 1:16; 10:9–13)

Why would anyone avoid or refrain from regular time reading the Word of God? As we have already seen, Satan hates our faith and will use any tactic to distract, deny, or delay our time in Scripture. Satan will try to convince us that we don't need it—or God, for that matter. The Bible is called the Word of Truth, whereas Satan is called the Father of Lies. And we desperately need to know what is true during our walk of faith.

The Importance of Personal Time in the Word

For those of us who have been Christians for a while, we have heard much about devotions or quiet time. There are many excellent books and materials written to help us either get started or strengthen our time in the Word of God. Let me share with you how I have personally been helped. I have been in ministry for over thirty years and am now fifty-five years old. I have studied Scripture a lot to prepare over a thousand messages for speaking meetings, Bible studies, and chapels. I share that information because "preparing" for messages or studies is not the same as personally studying the Word. Don't misunderstand me—I have learned much from these preparations. I probably have grown and benefited from my preparation more than my listeners have from my talks. But even in the wonderful times of preparation, I was always thinking about delivering the message. Many years ago C. H. MacIntosh wrote to all of us who prepare studies for others:

> It is a very poor, yea, a very dangerous thing to sit down to the Word of God as a mere student, for the purpose of preparing lectures or sermons for other people. Nothing can be more deadening or withering to the soul. Mere intellectual traffic in the truth of God, storing up certain doctrines, views and principles in the memory, and giving them out with a certain fluency of speech, is at once deluding and demoralizing. We may be drawing water for other people, and all the while be like rusty pipes ourselves. How miserable this is. If any man thirst, let him come

> unto me and drink, said our blessed Lord. He did not say draw. The true spring and power of ministry in the church will ever be found in drinking for our own souls, not in drawing for others.[1]

In addition to time spent studying and preparing for ministry, I have benefited from practicing the following spiritual discipline. Several years ago, I began reading through the whole Bible once a year and the New Testament twice. There are several plans one can use, available in several books and at many Christian bookstores.

A Practical Suggestion

I've often read through the Bible chronologically, which has not only opened my eyes to the flow and background of Scripture, but also increased my joy and insight. Although Genesis describes the beginning with Creation and Malachi (the last book of the Old Testament) was written at the close of the Old Testament period, much of the Old Testament is not compiled chronologically. Its thirty-nine books are placed in groupings—the Pentateuch (Genesis through Deuteronomy), historical books (Joshua through Esther), poetical books (Job through Song of Solomon), and the prophetic books (Isaiah through Malachi). When I read chronologically, I find out which prophet was living during a certain king's reign and what letters were written during a certain period.

The New Testament contains twenty-seven books, most of which are letters written to individuals or churches. This Testament can be categorized by the Gospels (Matthew through John, which contain primarily the life, ministry, death, and resurrection of Christ), The Acts of the Apostles (book of Acts, which is a record of the early church and the apostles' journeys), and the Epistles (Romans through Revelation, which are letters written to churches and individuals about God, salvation, and Christian living). A reason why it is beneficial to read the New Testament chronologically is that the history recorded in Acts gives us a timetable of when certain Epistles (letters) were written; therefore, we can read about the apostles' visits to certain locations along with the letters addressed to the people living there.

Reading chronologically helps me understand Scripture. In addition to this method, I use a different translation each year. The benefits of studying various versions of the Bible are great. For instance, if you are like me, your Bible is all marked up. Perhaps you even remember on which side of the page a certain verse is located! I like to take a different version each year and mark it up. I have a Bible that I use the most, but I like to read others for fresh perspectives. Some of the versions my wife and I have used are the *New International Version, New American Standard Bible, New Century Version, New Living Translation, Amplified Bible, New King James Version, The Message,* and *God's Word.*

If reading through the complete Bible is too much to begin with, the New Testament is a good place to start. The key is getting the Word of God into us, which starts by opening the Book. Then we need a plan. But, most importantly, we must pray that God will open our hearts to what we are reading. An English evangelist, Gypsy Smith, used to say, "What makes the difference is not how many times you have been through the Bible, but how many times and how thoroughly the Bible has been through you." There are various reading plans and chronological Bibles available. Why not give it a try?

Going Deeper

After establishing a daily reading plan of, for example, two to three chapters a day, you might want to set aside one day a week for more intensive study, such as going over verses you've heard in a message or further study of a topic brought up in a group setting. Another possibility is to study a specific book of the Bible or certain subject, such as names of God, festivals in the Old Testament, or even a biblical character. Some helpful tools are study Bibles, concordances, Bible dictionaries, and devotional books. I have over five thousand books in my library, but if I spend more time in a book that is not Scripture than I do in the actual Word of God, I will be receiving the Word of Truth through someone else's filter.

A few years ago, my wife and I were overseas attending meetings held during the cricket World Cup. To many Americans, cricket seems like a silly sport. But for much of this world, including 1.1 billion people, cricket is serious. One afternoon when we were in between meetings, I was invited to play cricket with the local team. What an adventure! I have some athletic skills, but I confess that I really didn't know what I was doing. I was in no way prepared for the game of cricket. Can you guess the analogy coming? The Bible is our playbook that prepares us for the game of life and, more specifically, the battle of faith. We must go onto the field prepared to encounter numerous situations and challenges.

chapter eight

Armed for Conflict

Finally, be strong in the Lord and in his mighty power. Put on the full armor of God so that you can take your stand against the devil's schemes. For our struggle is not against flesh and blood, but against the rulers, against the authorities, against the powers of this dark world and against the spiritual forces of evil in the heavenly realms. Therefore put on the full armor of God, so that when the day of evil comes, you may be able to stand your ground, and after you have done everything, to stand. Stand firm then, with the belt of truth buckled around your waist, with the breastplate of righteousness in place, and with your feet fitted with the readiness that comes from the gospel of peace. In addition to all this, take up the shield of faith, with which you can extinguish all the flaming arrows of the evil one. Take the helmet of salvation and the sword of the Spirit, which is the word of God. And pray in the Spirit on all occasions with all kinds of prayers and requests. With this in mind, be alert and always keep on praying for all the saints. (Ephesians 6:10–18)

I was on a flight headed for meetings in the Midwest, and a young man sitting next to me pulled out his laptop to watch a DVD. I glanced over and saw he was watching *The Lord of the Rings: The Fellowship of the Ring.* A fight scene between the forces of good and evil caught my eye. It was an intense battle with several casualties. Clanging swords, blood, sweat, and tears were profuse.

I returned my gaze to what I was working on, still thinking about that battle scene. J. R. R. Tolkien created a world of good and evil in his epic three-volume work *The Lord of the Rings.* Director Peter Jackson did an excellent job in bringing the intensity of the fights and battles to the screen. I can't imagine someone on that battlefield without weapons and armor—they would be doomed. I'm sure you know where I am going with this, for we are in a battle every day of our lives. It is fierce, and the enemy is relentless. As we have discussed earlier, he and his minions attack our faith. The shocking thing is that each day countless numbers of Christians go on the battlefield without armor or weapons.

The Seriousness of Being Equipped

We somehow think that ignorance or intending to stay on the outside will protect us or somehow make us exempt from the battle. But we are engaged whether we like it or not. We have a foe that hates Christ and all of His followers. He is merciless, and he doesn't care if we are tired, have had a bad day, trouble upon trouble, or are just unprepared. He will take the battle to us. He knows the only way to get at God is to get at our faith. He would rather attack our faith and damage our confidence in God than cause our physical death (although this would only be through God's permission). Remember this: God has invested us with His reputation. We, as weak vessels, have the awesome privilege of displaying trust in an all-mighty God before a watching universe. "His intent was that now, through the church [that's you and I], the manifold wisdom of God should be *made known to the rulers and authorities in the heavenly realms*" (Ephesians 3:10).

We need not fear Satan, and we can be assured that his doom is certain. According to God's eternal wisdom, Satan is allowed to wage war with us, and we must be prepared for that battle or we will lose our witness before a watching world and universe. For a long time now, God has impressed upon Bev and me the importance of putting on the armor of God, and we feel so strongly about this that we do not want to launch our day without it. I must be quick to say that this is not some mantra to be chanted repeatedly, nor is it a religious talisman to be used. Just repeating the verses that contain the armor of

God is not enough. There has to be heartfelt prayer associated with it. There needs to be flat-out dependence on God, with a desire to live a life pleasing to God. We know that "apart from [Christ we] can do nothing" (John 15:5). So in humble dependence on God, and with hearts of faith, we believe God and obey Him in putting on the *full* armor of God.

Putting on the Armor of God

Let's look specifically at what the Bible says about putting on the armor of God. The verses in their entirety are listed at the beginning of this chapter. The order of putting on the armor is not what is important, but the putting on the entire armor is crucial. For the sake of illustration, let me share with you my personal practice. I first put on the *belt of truth*. This is a great reminder of the necessity of worshiping the God of all truth, being led by the Spirit of truth, and lifting up Him who is the way, the truth, and the life. I am also reminded that God's Word is truth. This belt prepares me for the attacks of Satan, who is the Father of Lies.

Next I put on the *breastplate of righteousness*. This reminds me that I have righteous standing before God, but also that I am called to live a holy and righteous life. I am to love God with all my heart, so I want to protect my heart with this breastplate, lest I love the things of the world.

Following the breastplate, I put on the *shoes of the gospel of peace*. These are troubling days, and it would be easy for me to lose heart and become faint. Christ has promised His peace to guard and rule my life. I also put on these shoes because I am called to proclaim peace that is available to those who are far from God. I am Christ's ambassador.

Next comes the *helmet of salvation*. Proverbs 23:7 (NASB) tells us that "as [a man] thinks within himself, so he is." If there is any area Satan loves to assault, it is our minds. We need to protect our minds from Satan and the world's influence. Therefore, we think about eternal things, of others and not only ourselves, and put on the mind of Christ (Colossians 3:1–3; Philippians 2:3–4; 1 Corinthians 2:11–16). As we are told in 2 Corinthians 10:3–5, "For though we live in the world, we do not wage war as the world does. The weapons we fight with are not the weapons of the world. On the contrary, they have divine power to demolish strongholds. We demolish arguments and every pretension that sets itself up against the knowledge of God, and we take captive every thought to make it obedient to Christ."

After the helmet of salvation, I lift up the *shield of faith.* For me, this means that by faith I believe in His presence, His protection, His provision, and His plan. Satan continually hurls his darts of accusation my way. I must hold this shield high to block his attacks.

The next piece is the only offensive armor listed, *the sword of the Spirit.* Satan does not fear you or me, but he does fear the Word of God. It is important that I speak the Word of God. The word used here for *Word of God* is *rhema.* This Greek word means the "spoken word."

The last piece of armor is the "glue" to the entire weapons of our warfare. It is *praying all kinds of prayers in the Spirit.* It has been said that Satan fears the weakest saint down on his knees. Prayer moves the arm of God. We can accomplish more through prayer than anything. And notice that it says "all kinds of prayers." That means not just petitions and requests, but adoration, praise, thanksgiving, confession, and intercession.

MOODY'S COAT

Many years ago, the Lord gave me an usual opportunity and experience I will never forget. In the summer of 1988 while traveling in beautiful New England with my family, we stopped in Northfield, Massachusetts, to see D. L. Moody's home and conference center. Unfortunately, it was closed when we arrived. I was very disappointed and about to leave when I noticed a small house located next to the grounds. I decided I would see if anyone was home, and if they could give me some information on when it would reopen. I knocked on the door and an elderly gentleman answered. When I asked him my question, he looked at me for a moment and then at my family, and with a twinkle in his eye he said, "Would you like to see it now?" It turned out that he was the caretaker, and for some reason that only God knows, he took a shine to our family. I told him, "Absolutely," and thanked him profusely. I then experienced something I could never have imagined in my entire life.

First, he took us to Moody's home and birthplace. After walking through the house and seeing the various rooms, he lifted the velvet cord that kept tourists from entering certain rooms and asked if we would like to go into Moody's office. Wow, would we ever! He led us in and then said, "Take your time; look at everything." He had me sit at Moody's desk where I spotted Spurgeon's Bible, which Mrs. Spurgeon had given to Moody when Spurgeon died. I looked through it, seeing underlined words and notes off to the side. I sat in Moody's chair trying to imagine him studying there.

The caretaker had me try on Moody's jacket, which hung on a hook nearby. It was large, but what a thrill! "Why don't you look at his files and messages?" he asked. So I looked at his handwritten messages and pulled out several files. The caretaker must have loved every minute of this, since I acted like a kid in a candy store. My kids were getting a kick out of seeing their dad this way. I won't bore you with all the details of my experience, except to mention this last part. After viewing his gravestone, which was inspiring in itself as it was inscribed with some of Moody's own words, the caretaker took us to the conference center and auditorium. He brought us up onto the stage and platform and had me stand behind the pulpit. Then he left us alone. My wife and kids eventually went outside too. I looked down at the pulpit to read names of some great preachers who had spoken there during Moody's life. Many of them had written books that sat on my bookshelves at home! As I stood there, I cried out to God and asked that I would have passion and fire like these men.

Well, I certainly did not become a famous preacher or orator. Most of you probably were not especially familiar with the name on the cover of this book. That is not the point. You and I may never become famous. We may never affect our world in a way that is widely known; but like the saints of old, we can have a life of personal victory. Like Moody, Spurgeon, Morgan, and a host of others, we can win the battle. We aren't called to fill Moody's coat, but we are given the armor of God to equip us in the fight of faith.

Let's close this chapter asking God for the strength that only He provides: "O Thou whose every promise is balm, every touch life, draw near to Thy weary warrior, refresh me, that I may rise again to wage the strife, and never tire until my enemy is trodden down. . . . Give me a draught of the eternal fountain that lieth in Thy immutable, everlasting love and decree. Then shall my hand never weaken, my feet never stumble, my sword never rest, my shield never rust, my helmet never shatter, my breastplate never fall, as my strength rests in the power of Thy might."[1]

chapter nine

Trials, a Necessary Process

Not only so, but we also rejoice in our sufferings, because we know that suffering produces perseverance; perseverance, character; and character, hope. (Romans 5:3–4)

Our family really enjoys hiking and climbing, and we have done much of it not only throughout the United States, but also overseas. Our kids started when they were strapped to our backs and have never stopped. For the past few years, we have lived in Colorado at an elevation of 8,800 feet, where there are plenty of mountains. The closest "peak" to our home is Pike's Peak, one of the over fifty *fourteeners* (Coloradoans call their state's 14,000-foot-plus mountains *fourteeners*). The view at the top is spectacular. When we hike it, we start at a place called Manitou Springs; from there, the hike up is a seven thousand-foot elevation gain. It is strenuous, with several grueling sections of trail, and, for most climbers, parts are certainly not fun. To reach the top with its views, one must traverse jagged, rocky terrain. We cannot get there without a difficult and challenging climb.

We have been talking about the desire to have faith that pleases and, on occasion, amazes God. We've looked at the weapons that God has made available to us for the fight of faith. They are wonderful tools. Nevertheless, one of the greatest helps to our growth and confidence in God is not something we normally welcome. That help is trials. The truth of the matter is, we will never ascend the mountains of faith unless we experience and walk through the valleys of trials and hardships.

No Pain, No Gain

Years ago Amy Carmichael wrote these words, appropriate for understanding the importance of trials:

Hast thou no scar?
No hidden scar on foot, or side, or hand?
I hear them hail thy bright ascendant star:
Hast thou no scar?

Hast thou no wound?
Yet, I was wounded by the archers, spent.
Leaned me against the tree to die, and rent,
By ravaging beasts that compassed me, I swooned:
Hast thou no wound?

No wound? No scar?
Yes, as the Master shall the servant be,
And pierced are the feet that follow me;
But thine are whole, can he have followed far
Who has no wound, no scar?[1]

The verse at the beginning of this chapter reminds us that character development is dependent on trials and tests, or at least dependent on how we respond to them. In the same way, James 1:2–4 says, "Consider it pure joy, my brothers, whenever you face trials of many kinds, because you know that the testing of your faith develops perseverance. Perseverance must finish its work so that you may be *mature and complete,* not lacking anything." The word *trials* can include a wide range of experiences—some severe, some simply inconvenient. Trials can include sorrow, bereavement, suffering, difficulties, challenges, stretching, perplexities, silence, loneliness, confusion, and discomfort. The point is that a trial can be any size. We can be successful in handling a large one yet utterly fail with a smaller one.

Trials are tailor-made. They can include evil and temptation, which do not come from God, but He allows them, and they still fall under His sovereignty and control. If we are children of God, we will experience trials. There is no other way to grow in our faith (remember in quality, not size). The intensity and size of the trials will not make sense to us. Why do some people experience large trials and others smaller ones? Why do some seem to face repeated trials and others only on occasion? We must trust our wise and sovereign God in these matters. He not only knows what is best, but also He is loving and kind. I submit that, in heaven, when we see the final results of trials, we will have wished for more.

The Benefit of Trials

It is always risky to try to explain the reason for a specific trial, especially when it is someone else's experience. To complicate matters, Satan, who is the accuser of the brethren, loves to mess with our minds as we respond to trials. It is also true that some tests or trials will never be understood until we reach heaven. It is this very fact that makes trials so valuable to our faith. It is trusting God when life doesn't make sense. This is the highest form of worship.

In chapter 3, I quoted 1 Peter 1:6–7, which says our faith is more valuable than gold. These verses emphasize the value of the trying or testing of our faith. "In this you greatly rejoice, though now for a little while you may have had to suffer grief in all kinds of *trials*. These have come so that your faith—of greater worth than gold, which perishes even though refined by fire—may prove to be genuine and may result in praise, glory and honor when Jesus Christ is revealed."

The Old Testament character Job understood the value of trials and desired their results. "But he knows the way that I take; when he has tested me, I will come forth as gold" (Job 23:10). The greatest goal of trials is to develop our character and point to the sufficiency of God. We may not understand the immediate reason for a trial that seems to make no earthly sense—even seeming to be the opposite of what we would assume God wants to do—but trials are never wasted, and they are never haphazard.

The Bible talks about other purposes for trials. All of them fall under the main purposes of our growth and God's glory. Though we ought not be presumptuous by telling others "why" they are experiencing certain difficulties, we can share with them some biblical reasons for trials. Knowing this can be helpful and can often assist us in our own trials of faith. For the rest of this chapter and the next, I want to share with you ten possible reasons for the entrance of trials into our lives.

That We Might Share in Christ's Sufferings

We are probably all a bit guilty of only quoting Bible verses that we like. There is nothing wrong with that. We often pick passages that promise something desirable, such as comfort, health, wealth, significance, or another earthly blessing. One of the verses that I have quoted is Philippians 3:10: "I want to know Christ and the power of his resurrection" This is a great verse and ambition; however, there is more to the verse than that! Paul says he also wants to know "the fellowship of sharing in his sufferings, becoming like him in his death."

Now, that is a strange ambition! Share in His sufferings? Become like Him in His death? Why would someone desire that? One reason might be that when we suffer and experience trials of all sorts, it makes us appreciate how much Christ suffered on our behalf. Whether we suffer physically with illness, pain, or even torture, or suffer something emotionally like isolation, loss of a loved one, mental health issues, confusion, disorientation, loneliness, betrayal, and slander, we have a chance to enter into His sufferings. "During the days of Jesus' life on earth, he offered up prayers and petitions with loud cries and tears" (Hebrews 5:7). Trials may come so that we can identify with and appreciate what Christ voluntarily suffered for us.

That We Might Be a Testimony to the Sufficiency of God

Perhaps the most powerful demonstration to a watching world that God is real and personal is the grace of God in difficult times. To an unsaved world, suffering points to the supernatural because it does not make sense otherwise. We often think that success stories are the best testimonies. They can be powerful, and God has certainly used them. They can, however, create unhealthy expectations or even a spirit of discontent where people think, *I wish I could be like so-and-so.* The grace that God pours out amidst suffering and trials points not to the individual, but to the supernatural sufficiency of God. As Paul said, "Now I want you to know, brothers, that what has happened to me has really served to advance the gospel" (Philippians 1:12).

When a person is in a crisis, he or she may be asked: "How can you handle this?" or "What is your secret?" This is the opportunity to point to Christ and His sufficiency. One of those passages of Scripture we like to quote is Philippians 4:13: "I can do everything through him who gives me strength." This is a wonderful promise, but we sometimes remove it from its context. Permit an illustration of an incident that took place during one of the NBA chapels I was conducting. The National Basketball Association offers chapel before every game. Since there are so many chapels, I could actually teach a miniseries on certain Bible themes or topics. On one such occasion, I was sharing a series on God's sufficiency in trials, focusing on Philippians 4:11–13. I ended the last study by giving the players who were in chapel a laminated card with verse 13 on it. After chapel I walked into the locker room, and a player who was not in chapel approached me. "Hey Bruce," he said, "I'd like one of those cards." I shared with him that it was part of a chapel series, and it probably wouldn't make much sense to him. He insisted on having it. That night he went out and scored fifty points! He was unstoppable. After the game he called me over and said, "I had it in my shoe!" "What?" I said. He explained he had put the card in his shoe and it had empowered him to play well! Somehow, I don't think that was what the apostle Paul had in mind.

Here is what the verses say in their context: "I am not saying this because I am in need, for I have learned to be content whatever the circumstances. I know what it is to be in need, and I know what it is to have plenty. I have learned the secret of being content in any and every situation, whether well fed or hungry, whether living in plenty or in want. I can do everything through him who gives me strength." Paul said that in whatever situation we are facing, in whatever circumstance we are experiencing, God gives us the strength we need. In fact, Paul shared in 2 Corinthians 12:9 that the Lord told him, "'My grace is sufficient for you, for my power is made perfect in weakness.'"

I wish I had the time and space to share my observations of people who have persevered through deep pain and experienced such superabounding grace. I think of friends who lost their fifteen-year-old son to suicide, others whose nineteen-month-old son drowned, and friends who have lost jobs, health, and loved ones. My own father suffered, and eventually died, from Lou Gehrig's disease. By our faith and trust in God's sovereign plan we can, even with tears, reflect God's grace and sufficiency.

That We Might Be Able to Identify with Others in Their Difficulties and Hardships

A third possible reason for going through trials is to identify with others who face similar situations. In one sense, we are not individuals since in Christ we are all members of His body. God never planned for us to be lone rangers, but to be part of a living organism. The apostle Paul described what "body" life looks like in 1 Corinthians 12. Every Christian ought to spend time reading this chapter. "The body is a unit, though it is made up of many parts; and though all its parts are many, they form one body. . . . Now the body is not made up of one part but of many. . . . *If one part suffers, every part suffers with it;* if one part is honored, every part rejoices with it" (12:12, 14, 26).

Unfortunately, our natural tendency is to ignore or avoid our brothers and sisters in the family of God who are hurting. There can be several reasons for this; perhaps we are uncomfortable dealing with the suffering of others and don't know what to say or do. Maybe we think that if we ignore suffering that we ourselves can somehow escape it. When God permits or sends trials into our lives, we are suddenly more sympathetic to others. Our eyes and ears are opened to see and hear others. Like most of us, I have experienced trials of various sorts. As is often the case, when I see others' struggles, mine seem to pale in comparison. However, the trials that I have faced make me more sensitive to the pain of others. For instance, I recall seeing my father-in-law suffer with a bad back. I certainly loved him, but it was hard to empathize with what he was experiencing. Then when I hurt my back, everything changed! It was so painful and debilitating that I didn't know how my father-in-law and others like him survived!

That We Might Learn How to Pray More Intelligently for Others

One of the great opportunities God gives believers is to pray for one another. God has determined to use people's prayers in sustaining them and others in their difficulties. The church prayed for Peter (Acts 12:5), Job prayed for his three friends (Job 42:10), Epaphras prayed for his brothers and sisters at Colossi (Colossians 4:12), Moses prayed for Miriam (Numbers 12:13), and Paul continually prayed for the Christians in the churches he founded (Ephesians 1:16). When we experience trials, it makes us sensitive to those of others, and we therefore want to pray for them. Don't ever underestimate the value and mutual encouragement of praying for others. Paul stated that this is a priority. "I urge, then, *first of all,* that requests, prayers, intercession and thanksgiving be made for everyone" (1 Timothy 2:1).

Perhaps the trial you are experiencing has entered your life to encourage you to pray for *others.* Perhaps trials came into your life for others to be prompted to pray for *you.* Though the picture seems somewhat cryptic, the event that takes place in Revelation 8:3–4 is quite descriptive of our prayers: "Another angel, who had a golden censer, came and stood at the altar. He was given much incense to offer, *with the prayers of all the saints,* on the golden altar before the throne. The smoke of the incense, *together with the prayers of the saints,* went up before God from the angel's hand."

What a picture. God does hear our prayers. He is concerned. They come up before Him as incense (Revelation 5:8). He uses our prayers for others (James 5:15). In these days when our faith seems to be stretched to the limit, remember that there is a design to trials.

chapter ten

Trials, a Heavenly Intent

And we know that in all things God works for the good of those who love him, who have been called according to his purpose. For those God foreknew he also predestined to be conformed to the likeness of his Son, that he might be the firstborn among many brothers. (Romans 8:28–29)

No trials are wasted, for they have divine intent. Though there are many times when we do not understand, we can be confident that as we submit to the Father, He will ultimately use everything that happens for good. He has told us why there are trials, so that we might be conformed to the image of Christ and bring glory to God. We give God glory by *trusting* and *relying* on Him in difficult times. We become more like Christ and mature spiritually as we cooperate with the Holy Spirit.

The means to spiritual maturity is often an unwelcome guest. We must never underestimate the great lengths that God goes to in order to conform us to the likeness of His Son. It has been said that God is far more interested in our conformity than He is in our comfort. We often have it reversed, thinking that God is here to bless us with temporal things. Many of us suffer from this malady. From what the Word reveals about heaven, we learn that there will be no more opportunities to walk by faith once we are there. The processes of growth, conformity, and maturity must take place here on earth. That is not to say there may not be an expansion of knowledge throughout eternity, but there evidently will not be an ongoing process of transformation. Trusting God through our earthly life is of supreme importance for all of us since it directly affects our spiritual growth.

Let's continue looking at some of the purposes for trials found in the Word of God.

That We Might Honor God in the Presence of Heavenly Beings

We are earthly creatures. We have never seen heaven. All that we have experienced has been in this life. I touch, taste, hear, smell, and see the things of this earth. All of my senses have been programmed this way. When I became a child of God, I passed from death to life and became a new person in Christ, having new loyalties and affections (1 John 3:14; 2 Corinthians 5:17–18). My citizenship had changed, for I became a citizen of heaven (Philippians 3:20). I became a pilgrim, a sojourner traveling through a foreign country on my way home. To help me on this journey, God reminds me that what is around me is not as real as the place where I am going. "So we fix our eyes not on what is seen, but on what is unseen. For what is seen is temporary, but what is unseen is eternal" (2 Corinthians 4:18). It is challenging but imperative to fix our eyes on the things that are unseen, directing our thoughts and feelings above. "Since, then, you have been raised with Christ, set your hearts on things above, where Christ is seated at the right hand of God. Set your minds on things above, not on earthly things" (Colossians 3:1–2). When we develop life perspectives, we become aware of the bigger picture. Life is not all we see and not just "about me." There is a watching world—not just the visible one, but also an invisible one.

Even in our trials, "his intent was that now, through the church, the manifold wisdom of God should be made known to the rulers and authorities in heavenly realms, according to his eternal purpose which he accomplished in Christ Jesus our Lord" (Ephesians 3:10–11). A fascinating thought. Our lives, actions, and attitudes have an impact on the invisible world. We can display God's wisdom in the whole drama of redemption. The apostle Peter even mentioned that the angels are intrigued and "long to look into these things," as salvation's coming was predicted by the prophets and has now been revealed through Christ (1 Peter 1:12).

I am sure we can identify with the importance of seeking to respond to trials in accordance with God's will when others are watching or affected by it. Thinking about spirit beings watching us reminds us that they too can give glory to God because of our responses. Later we will look at the angels' observations of Job's trials. Much was at stake as a watching universe observed one weak man dealing with several trials.

That We Might Learn More About Ourselves

It is arguable as to whether blessings or trials teach us more about ourselves. Perhaps how we handle prosperity reveals more about us to others, whereas experiencing trials helps us to see ourselves more clearly. I may think I have grown in my faith and am doing quite well; however, when a trial hits and I don't respond how I had planned to when life was calmer, I realize how far I still have to go.

James writes in the New Testament about the man who looks in a mirror, then walks away and forgets what he looks like (James 1:23–24). Trials have a way of reminding us what we really look like. They help us remember that we all need to grow in grace (2 Peter 3:18). The Bible tells us that "we have this treasure [the light of Jesus shining in our hearts] in jars of clay [our frail earthly bodies] to show that this all-surpassing power is from God and not from us" (2 Corinthians 4:7). He gives us what we need as He lives through us, doing what we could never do alone, like causing us to have peace in the face of great trials.

The apostle Paul was honest about his own experience: "To keep me from becoming conceited because of these surpassingly great revelations, there was given me a thorn in my flesh" (2 Corinthians 12:7). That is not to say that each of us experiences trials because we are proud—it may be just the opposite. The humble believer desires more than ever to become the man or woman that God desires him or her to be. Humble people know that this can only happen by living a life of healthy self-evaluation with eternal perspective.

Trials remind us that the Christian life is not about self-sufficiency, but God sufficiency. We take Jesus' words to heart when He says, "apart from me you can do nothing" (John 15:5). It is not often that you'll find a "haughty sufferer." Tested people learn much about themselves and much about God's grace and sufficiency.

That We Would Learn Not to Focus on the Provision but on the Provider

Trials can be wonderful teaching tools that lead us to discover who God really is. Trials, for some, may drive them away from God as they become bitter, disillusioned, and confused. However, that does not need to be the case. Trials can be the pathway to new revelations and realizations about God. Sufferers often know God better than theologians and scholars.

There is something within all Christians that makes us aware that we were created for intimacy with God. But the "worries of this life, the deceitfulness of wealth and the desires for other things" distract us, and we seek our own agendas (Mark 4:19). Our relationship with God becomes one of seeking the gifts rather than the Giver. When God provides or supplies our needs, we often want more. (I often find this in my own heart. You may not struggle with this as much.) *Things* can replace our passion and desire for God. For example, many people were eyewitnesses to Jesus' life on earth. As the disciple John said of himself and his companions who had the Prince of Glory in their midst, "[We were with Him] that . . . was from the beginning, which we have heard, which we have seen with our eyes, which we have looked at and our hands have touched" (1 John 1:1). Imagine that!

Most people, however, were attracted to Christ because of what He could do for them. Jesus said of them, "Unless you people see miraculous signs and wonders, . . . you will never believe" (John 4:48). Later Jesus told them that they were looking for Him because He had given them bread (He'd actually just fed five thousand). Jesus went on to say, "I am the bread of life. He who comes to me will never go hungry, and he who believes in me will never be thirsty. But as I told you, you have seen me and still you do not believe. All that the Father gives to me will come to me, and whoever comes to me I will never drive away. . . . For my Father's will is that everyone who looks to the Son and believes in him shall have eternal life, and I will raise him up at the last day" (John 6:35–40). Though He offered them eternal life, when Jesus wasn't "doing things" for them but was talking about who He really was, many hated Him and even tried to stone Him (John 8:58–59; 10:30–33).

Trials can strip us so that all we have is God, and He is enough! He becomes our consuming passion. "One thing I ask of the LORD, this is what I seek: that I may dwell in the house of the LORD all the days of my life, to gaze upon the beauty of the LORD and to seek him in his temple" (Psalm 27:4). When we realize that Jesus is our only constant, we find that He is all we need.

Once we begin seeking God instead of His gifts, we see that God is drawing close to us. "The LORD is close to the brokenhearted and saves those who are crushed in spirit" (Psalm 34:18). James encourages us to "come near to God and he will come near to you" (4:8). The blessing of trials is intimacy with God.

That We May Begin to Grasp God's Mercy

Trials reveal God's mercy in several ways. By our responses to them, we often see that we have not grown as much as we had thought and that we really do have our own agendas separate from those of God. It is at such times that we can stop and revel in His mercy, seeing that it is He alone who redeems us from our fallen nature. We are undeserving, not meriting His kindness and forgiveness. We begin to learn how rich God is in mercy (Ephesians 2:4).

His mercy is revealed not only in the ways we find ourselves responding, but also as we begin to realize how bad the situation could be. We can always find people who are worse off than we are and imagine what it would be like to face their sorts of situations from the cradle to the grave. Fortunately, His mercies are new every day (Lamentations 3:23). God's mercy is also discovered in the way He comes to us, comforts us, and supplies our needs. As the psalmist says, "As a father has compassion on his children, so the LORD has compassion on those who fear him; for he knows how we are formed, he remembers that we are dust" (103:13–14). If it were not for trials, we would not know and experience as much of God's mercy.

That We May Begin to Grasp the Greatness of God's Sovereignty

For some, the sovereignty of God is a confusing and unsettling doctrine. It is not meant to be, because it is for our benefit and comfort. Our God reigns! "I make known the end from the beginning, from ancient times, what is still to come. I say: My purpose will stand, and I will do all that I please" (Isaiah 46:10).

There are no accidents or slipups with God. Nothing escapes His attention; nothing happens beyond His control or permission. "In him we were also chosen, having been predestined according to the plan of him who works out everything in conformity with the purpose of his will" (Ephesians 1:11). That verse could not be much clearer. We are not at the whims of circumstances or of Satan. I confess that I do not totally understand the sovereignty of God and that I will not fully understand it until I am in glory. Still, I believe that God is in control, and that brings me great comfort.

God has told us that He designed every day of our lives (Psalm 139:16), down to the exact times and places we would live (Acts 17:26). And God's sovereignty is coupled with His goodness and wisdom. He has our best in mind, and He will do that which will bring Him the most glory. Sometimes we can look back and see the wonders of God's sovereignty in this life. Other times it seems unclear. We can be assured, however, that the Master Craftsman has sculpted our situations—from financial setbacks to pain and physical limitations. Even sinful acts fall under the authority of the King of the Universe. The ultimate heinous crime committed in history was the crime committed against our Lord and Savior Jesus Christ. Peter understood God's sovereignty when he addressed the crowd that had turned against Jesus: "This man was handed over to you by God's set purpose and foreknowledge; and you, with the help of wicked men, put him to death by nailing him to the cross" (Acts 2:23). And yet the death and resurrection of Jesus Christ is arguably the world's worst crime that God planned to use for humanity's greatest good. Our sovereign God is still in control of our lives and the universe.

That We Might Long for Heaven

This point will be further developed in the final two chapters, but I will mention it here. Simply put, trials make us realize that this is "as good as it gets" down here. Every time we get comfortable, trials remind us that this is not a perfect world. Solomon had unlimited wealth, influence, possessions, and power. Yet he said that all of it was meaningless (see his thoughts on this throughout the book of Ecclesiastes).

There is nothing wrong with longing for heaven. God wants us to think about our eternal home. Paul suffered a lot, and yet he could say with confidence, "I consider that our present sufferings are not worth comparing with the glory that will be revealed in us" (Romans 8:18).

Growing up, I was the youngest of three boys on a farm. We had a wonderful home with parents who loved the Lord. If you ever saw the TV show *Green Acres,* you may appreciate my parents' relationship, as my dad was from Montana and my mom from England (although she grew up in the States). As I mentioned earlier, my father died of Lou Gehrig's disease when I was a young man. My mother developed a severe case of arthritis and psoriasis when I was born. Although she would not always be this way, the psoriasis would become so bad she would have to be in the hospital, often for long periods. She would have to sleep in plastic bags. Her arthritis became advanced to the point that her fingers and toes were crippled. I am sure that this was difficult and embarrassing for her. However, I never recall her complaining or wishing for something else or even saying, "Why did God allow this?" I do remember that she loved heaven and longed for it. She has been home there for a long time, and now she has a perfect body.

Our trials may be different than hers, but they are still real. We need only to remember that heaven will be a wonderful place where there "will be no more death or mourning or crying or pain" (Revelation 21:4). It will be a place of rest and unimaginable joy.

Trials prompt us to look toward home. Thinking of trials as one of the "helps" for our walk of faith seems strange. Still, we must remember that the trying of our faith can bring about much good.

chapter eleven

Faith the Second Time Around

Remember those earlier days after you had received the light, when you stood your ground in a great contest in the face of suffering. . . . So do not throw away your confidence; it will be richly rewarded. . . . "My righteous one will live by faith. And if he shrinks back, I will not be pleased with him."
(Hebrews 10:32, 35, 38)

I have already referred to one comic strip character in this book, and now I want to mention another. I guess this reveals to you what kinds of great theological works I read! The character, or I should say characters, are Frank and Ernest. They have found themselves in all kinds of situations, in various eras of time. Once they were in ancient biblical days, and Frank's character was holding a slingshot and talking with Ernest. In the background loomed a very large giant. Frank said to Ernest, "This is the hard part, having to defend the title each year!" What a great line as well as an accurate depiction of what each of us faces the second (third, fourth, and so on) time around in our walks of faith.

Does Faith Get Easier?

One would think that faith is easier the second time around, but it is not. I have noticed that the faith I've previously stood behind becomes more easily shaken as I face later trials, especially those that are similar to ones I have already experienced. It does not make sense, for I would think that once I have experienced a situation and seen God's grace, my faith would be bolstered so that I would trust God again in that trial. I cannot begin to tell you how many times God has led me through a difficult circumstance and I've said to Him, "I've learned from this. Next time I will not be shaken; I will trust you." Wrong! I find myself fretting, worrying, becoming anxious, or trying to work it out myself. When will I ever learn? Hopefully, I'm not as bad as I sound—hopefully. I pray that I may grow in my confidence in God. I have memorized some verses that I want to be true in my life, like Isaiah 30:15: "In quietness and trust is your strength" and Psalm 131:2: "I have stilled and quieted my soul; like a weaned child with its mother, like a weaned child is my soul within me." We even have those verses on our walls. I confess, however, that faith the second time around is still a challenge.

I do find comfort in knowing that I am not the only one challenged in this way. The Word of God says, "You're not the only ones plunged into these hard times. It's the same with Christians all over the world" (1 Peter 5:9 MESSAGE). Bible characters reveal their struggles with faith the second time around. Let's look at some of these men, illustrating an age-old challenge.

Abraham

God used Abraham to deliver his nephew Lot from overwhelming odds. Abraham, with 318 men from his own household, fought against and defeated the armies of four kings. Afterward, God said to him, "Do not be afraid, Abram. I am your shield, your very great reward" (Genesis 15:1). Later, Abraham moved to the vicinity of Kadesh and Shur in the Negev, ruled by Abimelech. Abraham lied by telling the king that Sarah was his sister. Why did he do that? Abraham said, "I said to myself, 'There is surely no fear of God in this place, and they will kill me because of my wife'" (Genesis 20:11). Abraham trusted God to help him fight against four kings but not against a small tribal ruler. Worse yet, this was the second time Abraham failed such a test (see Genesis 12). He kept thinking that he could help God out by lying, though God never called him to do that.

Moses

As Moses led the children of Israel through the wilderness, they ran out of water and cried against Moses and God. God told Moses to strike the rock and water would come out of it. Moses believed God, and water rushed forth (Exodus 17:1–7). Several years later, after experiencing intimacy with God and seeing one miracle after another, Moses failed to trust and believe God when they ran out of water again. God told him to "speak" to the rock, but he failed to trust God's "new" way of getting water and hit the rock. The Lord said, "Because you did not trust in me enough to honor me as holy in the sight of the Israelites, you will not bring this community into the land I give them" (Numbers 20:12).

Elijah

Elijah fearlessly confronted the wicked and dangerously powerful King Ahab. Elijah stood alone against 850 false prophets. As he faced the king and his army, he trusted in God for fire to come down from heaven to prove to the false prophets that Jehovah is God (1 Kings 18). He then killed all of Ahab's prophets. When word reached Queen Jezebel's ears, however, she threatened to kill Elijah, who fled into the wilderness! Scripture simply says, "Elijah was afraid and ran for his life" (1 Kings 19:3). Faith was harder the second time around.

KING ASA

Early in his career, King Asa faced an overwhelmingly large army. The Bible says that Zerah the Cushite marched out against him with an army of a million soldiers. In faith, Asa called upon the Lord, "LORD, there is no one like you to help the powerless against the mighty. Help us, O LORD our God, for we rely on you, and in your name we have come against this vast army. O LORD, you are our God; do not let man prevail against you" (2 Chronicles 14:11). The Lord responded to Asa's deep faith with a complete victory.

Years later, Asa faced another army, actually smaller than the previous one. What did Asa do? In spite of what God had done for him previously, he went out and trusted the power and might of another nation. The Bible says Asa took silver and gold out of the treasuries of the Lord's temple and hired the king of Aram to protect him. God was not pleased and sent the prophet Hanani to confront him. Hear the words of this prophet to Asa: "Because you relied on the king of Aram and not on the LORD your God, the army of the king of Aram has escaped from your hand. Were not the Cushites and Libyans a mighty army with great numbers of chariots and horsemen? Yet when you relied on the LORD, he delivered them into your hand. For the eyes of the LORD range throughout the earth to strengthen those whose hearts are fully committed to him. You have done a foolish thing, and from now on you will be at war" (2 Chronicles 16:7–9).

THE APOSTLE PETER

Peter's wavering took place over a few hours' time, if not less. When Jesus warned him and the other disciples about the dangers ahead of them that night, Peter said, "Lord, I am ready to go with you to prison and to death" (Luke 22:33). Peter actually backed up those words with bold action. When a large, menacing crowd threatened to take his Savior away,

Peter stepped forward and cut off the ear of the high priest's servant with his sword. Think about the courage that took. He was the only one to defend Christ. However, as we know, within hours of defending Jesus, Peter cowered before a servant girl and denied his Lord, not just once, but three times (Luke 22:54–62). He failed the test of faith the second time around. There are several illustrations, but I think we get the picture. Faith is difficult the second, or third, or hundredth time around. Why is this? Is there a reason for this universal problem?

We Tend to Forget

I believe there is a reason. The Israelites who followed Moses into the wilderness are the best examples I know of when it comes to weak faith the second time around. Psalm 106: 12–13 sums up their attitudes toward God: "Then they believed his promises and sang his praise. But they soon forgot what he had done." Did you catch that word in the second part of the verse? They "forgot." That says it all. They forgot and we forget. We are good forgetters. It seems as though no matter how many times God helps us or sees us through, we forget. A sobering exercise is to look up the word *forgot* or *forgotten* in a concordance. God levels this accusation at His people so many times!

- *You have forgotten God your Savior; you have not remembered the Rock, your fortress.* (Isaiah 17:10)
- *You deserted the Rock, who fathered you; you forgot the God who gave you birth.* (Deuteronomy 32:18)
- *When I fed them, they were satisfied; when they were satisfied, they became proud; then they forgot me.* (Hosea 13:6)
- *Does a maiden forget her jewelry, a bride her wedding ornament? Yet my people have forgotten me, days without number.* (Jeremiah 2:32)

It is a pattern revealed throughout Scripture. Over twenty times God says His people have forgotten, and it usually happens after He has blessed them.

Some religious leaders made one of the most ironic statements during Jesus' ministry on earth. "What miraculous sign can you show us to prove your authority to do all this?" (John 2:18). They asked this on more than one occasion, even after witnessing many of Jesus' miracles. In fact, at the close of his gospel account, John says, "Jesus did many other things as well. If every one of them were written down, I suppose that even the whole world would not have room for the books that would be written." The problem was not in the numbers of miracles but in the fact that they were forgotten.

It is not that God has not answered our prayers in the past. It is not that He hasn't helped us through difficult times. It is that we have forgotten. We need better memories! I mentioned looking at the times God says His people "forgot." An even more exhaustive study is to find all the times God admonishes us to "remember." There are well over one hundred such admonishments:

- *Remember the wonders he has done, his miracles.* (1 Chronicles 16:12)
- *Remember the former things.* (Isaiah 46:9)
- *Remember those earlier days.* (Hebrews 10:32)
- *Remember what you have received. . . .* (Revelation 3:3)

We need to remind ourselves to remember! Yet we can train ourselves to recount God's faithfulness throughout the ancient times up to today. We can reflect upon our own faith experiences of trusting Him and learning from Him.

Keep a Record of Our Faith Experiences

Begin by keeping a journal or diary. For years many speakers and authors have suggested this, and they are right, because a journal can be invaluable. Women may be more successful than men in this area as a whole, but men can master it too. God told Moses to write things down for Joshua to remember (Exodus 17:14). A written account of our walk with God and His faithfulness in our lives is a great deterrent to forgetfulness. I started a journal later in life and found it to be worth the discipline. Find a nice book that fits you, and begin writing about life events, lessons learned, promises discovered, or anything else you want to record. Begin with short entries, writing during a quiet time or at bedtime.

Discuss What Is Happening with Others

"Talk about them when you sit at home and when you walk along the road, when you lie down and when you get up" (Deuteronomy 6:7). Share your stories with others. The verse I just quoted says to do this as a family, especially parents with children, but it also applies to others. I love what Malachi 3:16 says: "Then those who feared the LORD talked with each other, and the LORD listened and heard." We do not tell our stories enough. That is why it is so important to have friends and not live in isolation. One of the benefits of telling others our stories is that they can remind us of them! As Scripture says, "Iron sharpens iron" (Proverbs 27:17). In addition, we are giving God glory when we share how He has provided for us or taught us in a specific situation.

Write Notes in the Margins of Your Bible

As you read Scripture and experience life, make notes about it in your Bible. If God gave you a promise in His Word at a specific time, write the date next to the verse. Record experiences you are going through next to appropriate passages of Scripture. This has been a great encouragement to me and has strengthened my faith.

Memorize Passages of Scripture That Relate to a Trial You Are Experiencing

As you pass through a trial, learn Scripture that will help you through it. "If your law had not been my delight, I would have perished in my affliction" (Psalm 119:92). When experiencing trials the second time around, you have God's Word in your heart and mind. You can quote it and meditate on it. Deliverance and strength will come.

Pray That God Will Remind You of Past Trials

It is helpful and healthy to ask God to bring to mind His faithfulness in the past. Be honest with Him. "God, I am struggling with this difficulty. Remind me of our experiences together in the past. Bring to my mind how we handled this before. Renew my mind." God will answer that prayer.

Faith the second time around can be very challenging. Yet we can learn from our past and from others who have responded well and those who have not. We do not have to fail repeatedly, but can grow in our confidence in God as we look to Him. As trials accelerate, think back upon God's faithfulness.

chapter twelve

What Should I Expect?

And what more shall I say? I do not have time to tell about Gideon, Barak, Samson, Jephtah, David, Samuel and the prophets, who through faith conquered kingdoms, administered justice, and gained what was promised; who shut the mouths of lions, quenched the fury of the flames, and escaped the edge of the sword; whose weakness was turned to strength; and who became powerful in battle and routed foreign armies. Women received back their dead, raised to life again. ***Others were tortured and refused to be released, so that they might gain a better resurrection. Some faced jeers and flogging, while still others were chained and put in prison. They were stoned; they were sawed in two; they were put to death by the sword. They went about in sheepskins and goatskins, destitute, persecuted and mistreated.*** (Hebrews 11:32–37)

A few years ago I scheduled a luncheon appointment with two athletes, a football player and a hockey player. I wanted to meet with them because I was concerned that they were embracing a belief that was both harmful to them and potentially harmful to others. In short, they had been taught and believed that God blesses everyone who comes to Him in faith. That blessing always manifested itself in some type of comfort, prosperity, or elevation in life. In other words, if you trusted God, He would make you a star and use you in a mighty way. If you were sick or injured, He would always heal you. They backed up their theology with a few verses. This is a particularly attractive doctrine to those in professional sports, and it goes something like this; "God has raised you up for such a time as this. You are to be a star for Him. People will see you, and you can give glory to God." This is an appealing belief system. Who does not want to be a star?

The problem, of course, is that not everyone can be a star. Many strong Christians "ride" the bench without much playing time. Ballplayers who love the Lord get career-ending injuries or injuries that keep them from operating at peak performance. The truth of the matter is that there are many unbelievers who are better athletes than some Christians. At one Christian sports conference, a minister "anointed" several athletes and pronounced that God was going to use these ballplayers to be "superstars." Several months later some of these athletes had been cut from the team, and others had been relegated to the bench. You can probably imagine what this did to their faith.

Are the Results Always the Same?

If faith is so pleasing to God, what can we expect when we trust Him? There are many promises in the Word of God, and the promises in the Old Testament seem to refer particularly to temporal or earthly blessings, such as promises of long life, multiple children, victory over enemies, and even some earthly prosperity. The New Testament does not encourage in the same way. Instead of earthly blessings and comfort, it points to fiery trials, as mentioned in previous chapters. "Do not be surprised . . .", "So that no one would be unsettled . . .", and "It has been granted to you . . . to suffer for him" are common admonitions (1 Peter 4:12; 1 Thessalonians 3:3; Philippians 1:29).

Jesus reminded His disciples, "If the world hates you, keep in mind that it hated me first. If you belonged to the world, it would love you as its own. . . . Remember the words I spoke to you: 'No servant is greater than his master.' If they persecuted me, they will persecute you also" (John 15:18–20). The Son of God was the most irreproachable person who ever walked the face of this earth. He always pleased His heavenly Father. And yet He was hated, betrayed, and crucified.

One of the most important things I can share in this book is this: the results of living a life of faith are varied—in this life. In the closing chapters of this book, I will talk about the tremendous rewards in heaven for living a life of faith. God will honor us in a way that is inconceivable and unbelievable. But for now, God's rewards and the results of living by faith will be varied. And, to be honest with you, they (the results) will not always make sense. I love reading Hebrews 11. It has rightfully been called "Faith's Hall of Fame." Here are some great lessons about battles won, overcoming incredible odds, victory, victory, and more victory. Wahoo, bring it on! Yet when we read on to verse 35, we see what happened to some of the *others*. We don't really want to hear about the others such as those who didn't win, get delivered, or find escape or the answers in this life. We want to hear from the people described in the first part of the chapter. Sign them up for our conferences. Let them write books. Let's buy their tapes. But the *others?* I don't want to hear from them.

It is necessary, however, to hear about them. *We must understand that the results of trusting God in this life are not always rewarded in this life.* God will reward one day; we can be sure of that, probably so much so that we will cry out, "Stop, that's enough!" But here in this life we may not experience it. What makes it more confusing is that some may experience many blessings. God may choose to bless some here and now for their walk of faith. He does do that, and He has done it in the past. How and when He blesses is up to Him.

Bible Examples of Varied Results

A look at Scripture reveals this truth. Come with me for a few moments as we peer into the Word. The apostles Peter, James, and John have been referred to as the "inner three."

Christ spent three intensive years with these men. What would normally be expected from such men? Most of us would figure that God would give each of them long and fruitful ministries.

Peter and James were both arrested. James was beheaded a few weeks after Christ ascended to heaven, though God miraculously delivered Peter. John lived for many years after Peter died. All were members of the inner three, but they all experienced different results from following Christ. How about John the Baptist? Jesus said, "No one is greater than John" (see Luke 7:28). What happened to John? He had a very brief ministry and then was beheaded.

In the Old Testament, we also find varied earthly results of following God. Uzziah (also called Azariah) was a follower of Jehovah who didn't follow Him wholeheartedly yet reigned for fifty-two years. Josiah, who was totally committed to God, reigned for thirty-one years and died at the young age of thirty-nine. In fact, if we look through Hebrews 11 we can see various results of walking by faith.

Why do I share this? Because we must understand that the ways of God are mysterious. God can be completely trusted, but He cannot be completely understood. "Oh, the depth of the riches of the wisdom and knowledge of God! How unsearchable his judgments, and his paths beyond tracing out!" (Romans 11:33). "How great is God—beyond our understanding!" (Job 36:26).

Who can fathom why one person is spared from cancer and another dies? Who can understand why one person escapes a car accident and another does not? Can you explain why one Christian soldier dies in battle and another survives, or why one child is born healthy and another is not? The answer may have nothing to do with the amount of prayers offered or people's lack of faith. God may very well be extremely pleased with a person's faith and still choose to do something or allow something that does not make sense to that person—at least not now, but it will someday. People who share in these experiences will one day be greatly honored for their faith and perseverance.

The Balance Between Boldness and Submission

All of us have experienced, to some degree, not receiving what we had hoped for. Many of us can testify to a delay in receiving the answer to a prayer. God's timing often does not seem to coincide with ours. Pastor Jim Cymbala speaks to this issue: "Many of our struggles with faith have to do with timing. We believe, at least in theory, that God will keep his promises —but when? If the answer does not come as soon as we expect, fear begins to assault us, and then soon we are tempted to 'throw away [our] confidence.'"[1]

There is a "cautious balance" in responding to the delays or denials of God. As I have been saying throughout this book, there is a pleasing faith that trusts God and praises Him no matter what, answers or no answers. There is also a holy boldness and persistence that is pleasing to God. Remember the story of the *persistent* widow? Christ began that parable by saying that people should always pray and not give up. I believe the balance is that we pray until we think we no longer have the liberty to pray, the answer comes, or (and this does occur) it is no longer relevant to pray (such as when a loved one fighting in a war is taken home to heaven). Cymbala speaks to this issue of persistence: "When we seek God for answers, we must persevere in prayer, letting it build up day after day until the force of it becomes a mighty tide pushing over all obstacles."[2]

Dave Dravecky is a former all-star pitcher for the San Francisco Giants and the San Diego Padres. His arm was amputated because of cancer. Dave and his wife, Jan, run a ministry called Operation Hope. Dave and Jan have written some wonderful books, and they publish a journal called *The Encourager.* Dave shares these thoughts in his excellent book *Do Not Lose Heart:*

> When his children pray to him, God does hear and he does answer. Simply because God does not answer all of our prayers in the way we would like them to be answered does not mean that there has been no answer. We must remember that, just as a par-

> ent must sometimes say "no" to a child, so must God sometimes say "no" to us. . . . I have learned through my struggles that after I have brought a matter to God in prayer, I can release it and know that he is in charge of it. I do not have to worry about it anymore. Oh, I will continue to pray for that concern—Jesus also taught us we "should always pray and not give up"—but the answer, whatever it may be, is in his hands.[3]

In these days approaching the return of Christ, we must remember that not all lives of faith will yield the same results. But they will one day be rewarded.

chapter thirteen

Faith's Affirmation

Those who honor me I will honor. (1 Samuel 2:30)

I was recently speaking to a group of young couples on the topic of faith. During a discussion, one young man said, "I am a little troubled by the thought that God does not respond to our steps of faith. I believe God reveals Himself and His will when we step out in faith." I appreciated what this young man was saying. I believe that God does honor those who honor Him. And many of us can testify to the times when God made something so "clear" that it was unmistakable that He was in it. But I wonder if we can so easily define how God affirms and is present when we step out in faith. As I have mentioned, many believers experience what seems like a slowness and silence from God.

Two nights ago I received a call from a man who was going through some major trials. As I listened to him share these difficulties, I felt somewhat overwhelmed. He had experienced trial after trial and had not "heard" from God in quite a while. In fact, it seemed to him that when he sought to honor God and trust Him completely, God abandoned him. This man was not a new believer. He'd served God faithfully in many capacities. Near the end of the conversation, he said, "I am beginning to wonder if God just started the whole thing, has walked away, and now we are on our own." He said, "I don't want to believe that—but the jury is still out. I hope I'm wrong."

Does God Always Confirm Our Decisions?

We've talked a lot about trusting God in the dark, but what about those moments when we think God has made something so clear and then He seemingly disappears? We long for an affirmation or confirmation that we actually heard God clearly and are doing what He wants us to do. I am not talking so much about fiery trials (although we may experience them) but about the times when we lose sight of where God is. We thought we were following Him, and now we can't seem to find Him. Perhaps there are those who are reading this who felt strongly that God was leading them to a career change or a major relocation. Then, after the move or change, *nothing*. Perhaps there have been unexpected hardships or periods of confusion. Maybe new relationships have been difficult or our family members have not responded well to the change. You are asking questions, but they seem to fall on deaf ears. And this is at the very moment when you would think that loud, clear confirmation should be given.

Picture of God's Carrying Us

A few years ago, I began to study what the Bible says about God "carrying us." It was a fascinating study and one that challenged my walk of faith. I believe that by looking at the way God carries us, we will better understand the role of receiving "confirmation" in our steps of faith. Perhaps the concept of a "carrying God" is new to you. The Bible clearly talks about how God carries us. From the book of Isaiah: "In all their distress he too was distressed, and the angel of his presence saved them. In his love and mercy he redeemed them; he lifted them up and carried them all the days of old" (63:9), and "Listen to me, O house of Jacob, all you who remain of the house of Israel, you whom I have upheld since you were conceived, and have carried since your birth. Even to your old age and gray hairs I am he, I am he who will sustain you. I have made you and I will carry you; I will sustain you and I will rescue you" (46:3–4).

How wonderful to know that we have a God who carries us. I am sure that several of us have the poem "Footprints" in our homes. We are truly blessed to have a God who carries us, but have we ever stopped to ask what that looks like? God said He carried Israel since their birth. What does that mean? From Abraham's time until the Assyrian Dynasty (when the two passages from Isaiah were written), there were some pretty rocky roads when they surely wondered if God was indeed carrying them. We tend to read passages of Scripture and not think of these people as being real. Were they like us? J. Oswald Sanders writes, "Our proneness to attribute almost superhuman qualities and sanctity to men of the Bible is a profound mistake and is contrary to the reiterated teaching of the Bible itself."[1] These were real men and women who waited on God.

God uses three specific analogies to describe how He carried Israel and how He will carry us. The three are: *as a father carries his child, as a shepherd carries his sheep, and as an eagle carries its young.* These three pictures can help us understand God's role in visibly affirming and confirming our walk of faith.

As a Father Carries His Child

"There you saw how the LORD your God carried you, as a father carries his son, all the way you went until you reached this place" (Deuteronomy 1:31). As I was typing this chapter, I received a phone call from our oldest son, Jeremy. His wife,

Wendy, is three months pregnant, and they were calling from the doctor's office to share their excitement at seeing the ultrasound. It's hard for me to imagine that my son is going to have a child. Was it really that long ago when my wife was pregnant with Jeremy? We have such special memories after the birth of each of our children, when we carried our sons and daughter close to our hearts, creating a special bond between us. Before they could walk, we carried them a lot. As they grew a little older, we held them less, but there continued to be times when they would reach for us to pick them up. If we were hiking or climbing a mountain, I would carry them over difficult terrain or over long distances.

Think of the times when God has carried you like a father. How special and needed this can be. I love Zephaniah 3:17: "The LORD your God is with you, he is mighty to save. He will take great delight in you, he will quiet you with his love, he will rejoice over you with singing." When I think of that verse, I think of a father singing over his child, quieting him. A verse quoted earlier, in chapter 11, uses the parent/child analogy: "I have stilled and quieted my soul; like a weaned child with its mother, like a weaned child is my soul within me" (Psalm 131:2). Jesus taught us much about the fact that God is our Father, for we have been born into God's family and have a special child/parent relationship. The Word of God reveals the Spirit of God inside of us and cries "Abba! Father!" Abba is a term of endearment, like saying "daddy" or "papa."

I believe that all of us have been carried as a child by his father. But we probably experienced it more in the early years of our salvation experience. God does still carry us this way from time to time—praise His glorious name!—but He doesn't always carry us like this, for as we grow in Him, we experience other types of carrying.

As a Shepherd Carries His Sheep

"He tends his flock like a shepherd: He gathers the lambs in his arms and carries them close to his heart; he gently leads those that have young" (Isaiah 40:11). In our culture, it is hard to imagine the relationship that a shepherd has with his sheep or lambs. It was more than a business with him, because a shepherd got to know his sheep. Jesus told the story of how the shepherd left his ninety-nine sheep to find the one lost one (Luke 15:1–7). The Old Testament reveals that a shepherd will lay down his life for his sheep, as David killed a lion and a bear to protect his sheep (1 Samuel 17:34–36). And of course, we have a wonderful picture in Scripture of Jesus being the Good Shepherd who gives His life for His sheep, like you and me (John 10:1–18; Hebrews 13:20–21).

Shepherds did not always carry their sheep, but on occasion they would. Sometimes a shepherd developed such an attachment to a particular sheep that he took it home as a pet, carrying it in his arms. Two other occasions might cause a shepherd to carry a lamb. One was when the lamb could not keep up and the shepherd would lift him in his arms and help him over difficult terrain or along a lengthy journey. Another time was when the lamb continued to stray, and the shepherd would actually need to discipline the lamb, sometimes even breaking his leg. He would then carry the lamb in his arms until he was healed. After that the lamb did not want to leave the shepherd's side. If you have been saved for any length of time, you have experienced Christ carrying you as a shepherd carries a lamb. He is called the Good Shepherd, the Great Shepherd, and the Chief Shepherd.

As an Eagle Carries Its Young

"Like an eagle that stirs up its nest and hovers over its young, that spreads its wings to catch them and carries them on its pinions. The LORD alone led him; no foreign god was with him" (Deuteronomy 32:11–12). This example used to depict God carrying us is the most graphic. The verse describes it well, but in case you missed it, let me help you understand this picture. You may know that eagles tend to build their nests high off the ground, in the tops of trees or in the mountains. When the parent eagles think their young are ready to fly, they give them some incentive by tearing up the nest (i.e., the parent "stirs up the nest"). The eaglets are startled when Dad and Mom destroy the nest. They back away from the edge, but the disruption continues. Eventually the eaglets are forced to jump or fall out of the nest. This is rather frightening—actually, terrifying! The babies fall, but the parents swoop down, spread their wings, and catch them. The parents literally carry them on pinions (the flight feathers of the wings). What a picture of carrying. Now, of the three examples of God's carrying us, which would you choose? Kind of a no-brainer, right?

Let's go back to the beginning of this chapter. We were talking about our desire for God to make clear His will for our lives, which He sometimes does, making us feel His presence so closely. We can almost hear His heart beating as we press our heads against His chest, for He is carrying us as a father carries his child. In other instances, He carries us as a shepherd carries his lambs, though it may not always be for the best reasons. Perhaps we are tired, or we can't keep up, or we have been stubborn and rebellious; but God still loves us. He died for His sheep, and He will tenderly carry us. Here is the point, however, that we must not miss. Sometimes His carrying can be a frightening experience, such as when an eagle carries its young. He may disrupt our "nest" (our comfort zones), and seem to allow us to fall, while we wonder, *Where is God, and when will He rescue me?* I believe this type of carrying is necessary for us to "spread our wings." God has designed and desires for us to "soar on wings like eagles" (Isaiah 40:31). But it is hard to get us out of the nest!

LIKE DOVES OR EAGLES?

God will answer our prayers, and He will come through for us according to His will and His timing. But will I be willing to allow Him to carry me like an eagle? Will I be willing to fall and be caught at the last minute? Will I be willing, as those young eagles are, to trust my heavenly Father even though He seems as if He is doing something that can be destructive in my life? We might think,*Well, who wouldn't want to be an eagle?* The truth of the matter is that most of us would rather be doves. Can you identify with the psalmist who said, "'Oh, that I had the wings of a dove! I would fly away and be at rest—I would flee far away and stay in the desert; . . . I would hurry to my place of shelter, far from the tempest and storm" (Psalm 55:6–8)? Did you catch that: "Far from the tempest and storm"? While doves must hide from the storms, eagles soar above the storms, even using the wind currents from the storms to lift them higher. That is God's desire for us.

Proverbs 3:5–6 reads, "Trust in the LORD with all your heart and lean not on your own understanding; in all your ways acknowledge him, and he will make your paths straight." Will God really do that? Will I always know which way to turn? Will I always hear His voice? It may be that we will find ourselves being called on to trust God even when we do not have constant confirmation. We may find that we will need to trust His heart when we cannot see His hand. We may be surprised at how many of the saints of the Bible trusted God's call in their lives, and then endured long periods of time without hearing from Him. So if we think that we are alone in this, we need to be of good courage, for we are not alone. In the next chapter, we will look at experiences of some of the great people of faith to see what they discovered to be the affirmation of their faith decisions. In fact, we will learn the most from the man God called the "father of all who believe."

As we seek to fight the good fight of faith in the days before the second coming of Christ, it helps to know that God will carry us, but this carrying may not always be in the manner we anticipated.

chapter fourteen

"He Was Here a Minute Ago"

By faith Abraham, when called to go to a place he would later receive as his inheritance, obeyed and went, even though he did not know where he was going. (Hebrews 11:8)

Have you ever tried to follow directions while traveling in a car? After you have gone one way for a little while, do you begin to wonder if you really saw the last sign? Perhaps the landmark was a fork in the road, or a large rock, or a railroad track. It is amazing that we can be so certain that we have passed a landmark, but after traveling for a while and not finding the next one, we begin to doubt if we really did see it. My wife, Bev, claims that I am notorious for panicking too soon. I'll say, "Maybe it wasn't the mark back there, because we haven't come upon the next one yet." She generally replies, "Just be patient; it probably is still up ahead. You've been following the directions." This sort of thing is frustrating while you are trying to find your destination. If it happens when you are seeking to determine the direction of your life, it can be downright frightening—and totally confusing.

When We Were So Certain We Heard from God

As I mentioned in the previous chapter, there are many out there who believed they "heard from God" about a certain direction or decision, and then, after stepping out in faith, they received little or no confirmation. Perhaps this was exacerbated by troubles or conflicts that appeared. They began to wonder if they really did hear from God in the first place. And if they did, might they have misunderstood?

I realize that some of you are uncomfortable with what I just wrote. Perhaps you believe that God will always go before you or any believer as a cloud by day and a pillar of fire by night—not literally, of course, but with that kind of clear confirmation. Let me say once again that there are certainly times when God wonderfully confirms our decisions. But does He do that all the time? Where does faith come in? We have emphasized over and over again that we are called to walk by faith and not by sight. God can certainly do anything, including causing a sheep's fleece to be dry when the ground is wet. But does He always do that, and does He desire to do that?

In looking at the good fight of faith, we can see that we may face some unique challenges in the days leading up to the return of Christ. This is not to say that it hasn't been hard in the past, but it will be especially so before the Second Coming. Nothing is as pleasing to God as our faith, and faith must be able to operate without needing visible evidence (remember, "certain of what we do not see"). This does not mean that faith is unreasonable, although it may seem to be on some occasions. Therefore, in the area of God's leading, there certainly can be times when God calls on us to believe Him in faith even when we do not see evidence of His presence.

Several men and women written about in the Bible have believed they heard the call of God and stepped out in faith, only to be struck by second thoughts and seasons of doubt. Again, we must remember that these were real people like us, having struggles like ours. I will list a few of them, in no particular order, and then focus in on one. The amazing thing about each of them is that, by and large, these people actually heard God speak to them. Think about that! They heard the voice of God and still doubted. In some cases, they saw God perform miracles. But for each of them, when God seemed silent, they struggled in their faith, and in some cases acted in ways that displeased God and made them poor representatives of Him.

Moses

Let's look at Moses first (Exodus 2). Most people believe Moses got his "first call" at the burning bush to deliver the Israelites, but the book of Acts seems to indicate that God had called him much earlier, when he was still a favored son in Egypt, having been rescued as a baby by Pharaoh's daughter. Acts 7:25 shows us that "Moses thought that his own people would realize that God was using him to rescue them" when he killed an Egyptian who was mistreating one of the Israelite slaves. But afterward, Moses had to flee into the desert because Pharaoh wanted to kill him. Moses thought he heard God's call for him to be an emancipator of His people at an early age, but when he thought he was acting to rescue them, God was nowhere to be found. Moses heard nothing, so he fled.

The Israelites

In Judges 20, one of the more obscure passages of Scripture, the Israelites are called upon by God to unite and attack one of their own tribe, the tribe of Benjamin. In verse 18, God instructs them to fight the Benjaminites. They did, and the Israelite army suffered twenty-two thousand deaths. They wept before the Lord and asked again if they should attack the tribe of Benjamin. The Lord told them yes (verse 23), so they attacked again, losing eighteen thousand soldiers. Can you imagine this army's confusion? They heard God's call, but then everything went wrong. What was God doing? Why did He not confirm His directive? They did eventually defeat the Benjaminites on the third try.

David

In 1 Samuel 16, the prophet Samuel finds David and anoints him king. For the next several years, David dodges Saul's spear as he flees for his life. You probably know the rest of the story, but David had to live through all those years wondering what God was doing and why God ever said he would be king.

Joseph

How about Joseph? God told him twice in two different dreams that he would one day be a ruler and that his family would be subject to him. Yet he was sold into slavery and eventually cast into prison. It was not until seventeen years after his dreams that Joseph was placed as a ruler in the court of Pharaoh. Don't you think Joseph struggled with believing that his first call was real? It sure looked like it wasn't going to happen. Evidently, God was not letting him in on what He was doing.

Abraham, Father of the Faithful

We could list several others, but the one I want us to focus on is the man who was called the "father of the faith." Abraham's name appears 315 times in the Bible, and over 75 times in the New Testament. Again and again the Bible highlights Abraham's amazing faith:

> *Against all hope, Abraham in hope believed and so became the father of many nations, just as it had been said to him, "So shall your offspring be." Without weakening in his faith, he faced the fact that his body was as good as dead—since he was about a hun-*

> *dred years old—and that Sarah's womb was also dead. Yet he did not waver through unbelief regarding the promise of God, but was strengthened in his faith and gave glory to God, being fully persuaded that God had power to do what he had promised.* (Romans 4:18–21)

That is quite a statement about this man's faith. Think about all the times he exercised great faith. When he was called to leave the city of Ur, he had no idea where he was to go or what to expect. He wouldn't be moving into a city, but he would be a perpetual nomad. Though all of the Promised Land was given to him, he never owned a piece of it until he bought a burial plot for Sarah. He was told he would be the father of many nations and that his offspring would outnumber the stars in the sky and the sand on the seashores—but he was an old man when God told him this, and his wife was barren! After his wife finally gave birth to Isaac and he had enjoyed a close relationship with his son, he was told to put him to death, a command that flew in the face of God's character and promises. What a life Abraham lived!

When God Seems to Withdraw His Presence

Abraham, like many others, faced what seemed to be contradictions as to how to proceed. God spoke clearly at the start; then He seemed to withdraw His presence. Abraham wandered about as a pilgrim, never really settling on a home. In fact, it wouldn't be until about 450 years later that his offspring would finally inhabit the Promised Land. During the years of wandering, Abraham experienced trials and stretching of his faith. Twice he lied about his wife being his sister because "there is surely no fear of God in this place" (Genesis 20:11). While waiting for his wife to become pregnant, he gave in to expediency and had a child with Hagar. God seemed so silent after giving him a promise for a son. Did he really hear God right?

Did God want him to take action himself and enter the bedroom of his wife's handmaiden?

Just because men and women are mentioned in Scripture does not mean that they didn't struggle with waiting on God when He seemed silent. So if God had the father of our faith go for a lengthy period of time without some affirmation of His promises, don't you think that we might experience that as well? Their stories can be an encouragement to us.

But why does God make us wait? As we have been saying all along, God has chosen the way of faith for us. It is the highest form of worship to trust God even when we can't seem to find Him. Abraham acted in great faith by believing God and leaving Ur and initially believing God about a son. It was amazing faith when Abraham continued to trust God in the trenches over the long haul. Yes, there were some setbacks and times of defeat. Abraham was human and struggled as any of us would, but he was growing in his confidence in God. When the ultimate test came for him to trust God, he believed, and his belief went down on record as the greatest act of faith recorded in history. I am speaking, of course, about his obedience of being willing to offer his son, Isaac, as a sacrifice on Mount Moriah.

A Great Act of Faith

Think about that act of faith. God had told Abraham repeatedly that He would fulfill His promises through his offspring, beginning with Isaac. Then these brief words came from God to Abraham: "Abraham . . . take your son, your only son, Isaac, whom you love, and go to the region of Moriah. Sacrifice him there as a burnt offering on one of the mountains I will tell you about." That was it! God said just those few words. And what was Abraham's response? "Early the next morning Abraham got up and saddled his donkey. He took with him two of his servants and his son Isaac" (Genesis 22:1–3).

This act of faith and obedience is almost beyond comprehension. How could he make himself do such a thing? Think of that journey to Moriah. God never spoke to him on the way. He never said, "This is only a test." Abraham walked on in silence. Even as he bound his son on the makeshift altar, hot tears streaming down his face, God remained silent. Again we ask ourselves, how could Abraham do this? The New Testament tells us how. "Abraham reasoned that God could raise the dead" (Hebrews 11:19). You see, Abraham had come to know his God. Though none of this made sense and God remained silent, Abraham would trust God above reason and circumstances. Abraham believed God's promises about blessing through his son Isaac. Abraham knew his God was too loving to hurt him in this way. So he believed something that no one else had ever believed before—that God could raise his son. As the knife is raised back, ready to plunge into the heart of his beloved son, God yells, "STOP!" Abraham went the distance and trusted God right to the end. Like that eaglet that fell from the nest, God swooped down and caught him at the last minute.

We Must Be Prepared

Will we experience times when God seems to withdraw after we've heard His call so clearly? We will if we want God to stretch our faith. As God was glorified when Abraham trusted Him, He is glorified when we go the distance in trusting Him. Yet I cannot close this chapter without reminding myself, and each of us, that we face dangers when we haven't heard from God in a while. We may be tempted to listen to the Evil One who would suggest that we utilize "creative alternatives" to accomplish God's plan. Many people have believed that they knew God's will and heard His voice, but they fell away when they didn't hear Him for a while. Abraham slept with his wife's handmaiden, seeking to bring about the promised child. For King Saul, it was going ahead with a sacrifice when Samuel was running late (1 Samuel 13:7–11). Achan (Joshua 7) went into the tent to take the plunder before he was allowed to do so.

One thing seems abundantly clear: God is the God of "wait." It is not that God has trouble bringing about His plans and program. He knows that waiting is unnatural for us. It involves trust. Waiting has always been hard, but never more so than in this "instant" world. We have speed dialing, high-speed Internet, callback buttons and other telephone features so we don't have to punch the numbers in, remote controls so we don't have to walk to the TV, and remote garage door openers so we do not have to get out of the car. The list goes on and on. Our trust need not wane when we are waiting. The Bible says, "They that wait upon the Lord shall renew their strength" (Isaiah 40:31 KJV). Our confidence and faith can grow and expand as we wait on God. "I wait for the LORD, my soul waits, and in his word I put my hope. My soul waits for the Lord more than the watchmen wait for the morning" (Psalm 130:5–6). God never fails. He may not come through according to our time frame, but if we wait on Him, He will not disappoint us. God says, "I am the LORD; those who hope in me will not be disappointed" (Isaiah 49:23). When we wonder *Where did God go?* we can be assured that He is still with us.

chapter fifteen

Where Should Our Confidence Be Placed?

I am not ashamed, because I know whom I have believed, and am convinced that he is able to guard what I have entrusted to him for that day. (2 Timothy 1:12)

Seeing is believing" is a phrase that we have all heard. Obviously, for the Christian, this is not always true. Did you see the scene from the movie *Indiana Jones and the Last Crusade,* when "Indy" is nearing the last obstacle to finding the Holy Grail, and he is faced with a seemingly bottomless chasm? He must cross it, but there is no visible means to get across. He is told to believe that even though he cannot see a way to cross, he must step out in faith. Hesitating a moment, he steps out onto an invisible walkway spanning the chasm. When he takes that step, he finds that there is indeed an invisible bridge to support him. After crossing to the other side, he kicks a little dirt onto the bridge to see the way when he crosses back.

The Correlation Between Confidence and Faith

I wonder if that really describes our faith. "God, I will trust You; just give me a little help along the way, a little dirt on the bridge." Back in chapter 2, I said that faith has to do with focus. Faith is belief in the invisible God. Faith is also flat-out confidence in God. This is not an easy topic to address. For many people, when they say they have confidence in God, they mean that they believe He will do what He says He will do. That is good and right and biblical. Noah believed God that it was going to rain, and he built an ark. Joshua believed God that the walls of Jericho would fall down, so he had the priests blow their horns. Elijah believed God for signs to give the people that He existed, like fire and rain when Elijah called upon the Lord. Peter believed God when he was told he could walk on water, so he stepped out of the boat. Faith often means believing that God will "do" something He has said He will do.

However, faith is *more* than believing that God will do something, as wonderful as that is. The reason it is more is that we can sometimes be mistaken as to what God intends to do. I told you this topic was not going to be easy. Biblical characters may have had God speak directly to them, sometimes audibly and maybe visibly, but for the most part, we do not experience that. I am not trying to put limitations on God's speaking to us (as if I could do that anyway), but certainly, in this church age, God has primarily spoken to us through His written Word.

Without an "out loud voice" or an unmistakable "sign from heaven," how do we discern if God is leading us to trust Him in an important area? Certainly the Bible will speak to us, since it is the living and powerful Word of Truth. Praise the Lord that the Holy Spirit lives in each of us, bringing that truth to light. God uses His Word and His Spirit, plus He can definitely use circumstances, impressions, and the counsel of friends. But here is the important question I want you to ask yourself: *In what do you put your trust?* Do you put it in what you believe has been revealed to you? As I mentioned earlier, I think that is a part of faith. There are those times, however, when what you thought would happen does not happen. It may be a matter of timing (and it will still happen later), but on other occasions you may have believed that God was going to do something that He was not going to do. Hang with me on this. Perhaps you had confidence that God was going to do something with a job, a certain relationship, or even an illness. God does wonderfully assure His children on certain occasions, but the point is that *He wants you to place your faith and confidence in Him,* not in the thing you believe He has revealed.

Our Confidence Must Be in God, Not What We Think He Will Do

I believe that, in many ways, confidence in what we believe He has revealed to us and confidence in Him are closely related, but the confidence in Him must supercede the confidence in what we believe He will do. Again, the focus of our faith must be God. Remember Hebrews 11:6? "Without faith it is impossible to please God, because anyone who comes to him must believe that he exists and that he rewards those who earnestly seek him." Can we see it? There it is, in the right order. We first and foremost must believe in God. We must have confidence in Him. Then, even if we do not receive the things that we thought we would receive, we still believe in Him. I know that for some of us, this may be unsettling. Perhaps we think that if we back away from what we believed God was going to do, that would be lack of faith and would be displeasing to God. Or, worse yet, we may think that we are making allowances for God to fail, thus trying to "cover for God" so He doesn't "look bad."

Just because God doesn't do something that we thought He would doesn't mean that He is not worthy of our trust. A person may believe that God has revealed something to him, such as a job change, a college to attend, a vacation to take, or even that an illness is going to be healed. I don't know how that was made known, but most likely it was not through direct revelation. To some, it may have come through a certain passage of Scripture, a book, or a message in church. All those are legitimate, but the question is: Do we place our confidence in what we believe God has said, or do we place our trust and confidence in Him?

Has God "Dropped the Ball"?

The reason I think this is so important is that many people are losing confidence (not salvation) in God because they are not getting answers to prayers they believed they would receive. God seems to have "dropped the ball." Why hasn't He done what we believed He would do?

Let's look at a hypothetical situation, although in all likelihood, something along these lines has probably happened or will happen in your life. You read a Christian book that challenges you to "find your passion," to leave and step out in faith and trust God. You seek God's guidance and perhaps even His affirmation. You move your family to a different part of the country and seek to find a new job or a ministry. Days turn into weeks, then months. The savings account dwindles. Your kids have not adjusted well at school or church. *Where is God?* you wonder. Why did He lead you here? You felt so positive in the beginning. So many verses and circumstances seemed to verify what you believed you heard. Now here is where faith is put to the test. Where is your confidence? Is it in the call? Is it in what you believed to be true about the change you were making? Or better yet, is it in God Almighty?

The Relation of Confidence and Contentment

I believe that God is greatly pleased when our focus is on Him and when we believe in spite of circumstances, even the ones that seem to go in the face of what we believed God was going to do. It may be that God orchestrated or allowed the circumstances that we believed were so clearly of Him so that we would be "disappointed" in everything but Him. There is a wonderful passage of Scripture that addresses this issue, found in Philippians 4:10–12:

> *I rejoice greatly in the Lord that at last you have renewed your concern for me. Indeed, you have been concerned, but you had no opportunity to show it. I am not saying this because I am in need, for I have learned to be content whatever the circumstances. I know what it is to be in need, and I know what it is to have plenty. I have learned the secret of being content in any and every situation, whether well fed or hungry, whether living in plenty or in want.*

That passage is even more powerful when we realize what Paul was really saying. He said that he had learned the secret of being content. This idea of learning the "secret" has to do with being initiated into something secret. We must admit that for many of us, we are outside the secret society of the contented. Yet Paul said he had "learned" the secret. This Greek word for *learned* is not the same word or words that are used elsewhere in this passage. Earlier Paul used two different words for *learned* and *know.* One has to do with learning or knowing by experience, and one has to do with learning by observation. In this verse, the word *learned* has to do with God's revealing something. God had instructed Paul about contentment. Contentment means to be unaffected by outward circumstances. His contentment was in God and not on what was happening around him.

Now here is the importance of this passage. Paul said something that we may miss. The NIV says, "I have learned the secret of being content in any and every situation, whether well fed or hungry, whether living in plenty or in want." Notice the phrase "living in plenty or in want." In the KJV it is translated "to abound and to suffer need." The last parts of the phrases "plenty or in want" and "to abound and to suffer need" come from a combination of words that mean "to arrive too late" or "to be tardy." Did you catch what Paul was saying? Not only that he was content in all things, but that he had experienced times when God seemed to be slow or too late. Even the great apostle Paul struggled with what seemed to be delays in receiving answers from God—or perhaps answers that didn't make sense. Although he felt that way, his confidence in God did not waver.

Is God Ever Late?

To answer this question, let's look at an incident in Paul's life. Around A.D.55–56, Paul made a brief stop in the city of Corinth. He had recently finished up a successful three-year ministry in Greece in the city of Ephesus. His plans were to head to Jerusalem to take care of some business, then to go west, perhaps as far as Spain, to share the gospel where it had not yet been preached.

During that proposed trip, he wanted to visit Rome to strengthen the believers there. So while he was at Corinth, he wrote a letter to the believers in Rome (the book of Romans in our Bible). In that letter, Paul shared with the Romans his intentions about his proposed visit. Let's hear his heart and desires:

- *I pray that now at last by God's will the way may be opened for me to come to you.* (1:10)
- *I planned many times to come to you . . . in order that I might have a harvest among you.* (1:13)
- *But now that there is no more place for me to work in these regions, and since I have been longing for many years to see you, I plan to do so when I go to Spain. I hope to visit you while passing through and to have you assist me on my journey there, after I have enjoyed your company for a while.* (15:23–24)
- *I know that when I come to you, I will come in the full measure of the blessing of Christ.* (15:29)

- *Pray that I may be rescued from the unbelievers in Judea and that my service in Jerusalem may be acceptable to the saints there, so that by God's will I may come to you with joy and together with you be refreshed.* (15:31–32)

Here is the rest of the story of how Paul finally made it to Rome. The Jews in Jerusalem did not accept him. He was attacked by a mob, then arrested. After some time, he was taken to Caesarea where he was placed under arrest and suffered various trials for over two years. He was placed on a ship as a prisoner headed to Rome to stand trial. The ship was wrecked on the way, and after another year had passed, he eventually arrived in Rome as a prisoner. For at least another two whole years, he remained under house arrest.

Paul's hopes and expectations never came to fruition. He didn't go as a preacher, but as a prisoner. From the world's perspective, he did not arrive refreshed with the full measure of Christ's blessings. But do you know what? Paul was okay because he had learned to be content in all situations. His hope and confidence was in God, not in how he thought God would operate. Paul thought he knew God's timing and the way he would go to Rome, but he surrendered that to the Lord. *He made plans but kept a loose grip on them.* Paul ended up in prison, but it proved to be a powerful platform from which to share Christ and strengthen the churches. He wrote his "Prison Epistles" from there. Acts 28:31 tells us that "boldly and without hindrance he preached . . . Christ." In one of his letters, Paul asserted that "what has happened to me has really served to advance the gospel" (Philippians 1:12). He was glad to be able to share the gospel of Christ with the prison guards.

I May Be Wrong About What He Wants to Do, But Not Who He Is

Faith is exercising confidence in God. We may believe that we know what God wants and that we are following His leading. Regardless, we know our God and have confidence in Him. God may seem to come too late, or He may seem not to make sense, but we will focus on Him, learning to be content. Along with King David we can say, "I am still confident of this: I will see the goodness of the LORD in the land of the living" (Psalm 27:13).

We can say, "Lord, even if You allowed circumstances that I didn't anticipate, I will still trust You." God may be allowing us to experience disappointments in circumstances, so that our confidence is in Him alone. "Who among you fears the LORD and obeys the word of his servant? Let him who walks in the dark, who has no light, trust in the name of the LORD and rely on his God" (Isaiah 50:10).

chapter sixteen

Rock Solid About God's Love

How great is the love the Father has lavished on us, that we should be called the children of God! . . . There is no fear in love. But perfect love drives out fear, because fear has to do with punishment. The one who fears is not made perfect in love. We love because he first loved us. (1 John 3:1; 4:18–19)

I remember the first time I saw the Grand Canyon. For years people had told me how unbelievably magnificent and beautiful it was. As I walked toward the rim of the canyon, I kept telling myself to be ready to be awed. When I reached the canyon edge, I felt a "gasp" come up from my throat. I could not believe what was before me—it was beyond anything I had imagined!

I think that when we arrive in heaven there will be many "gasps" escaping from our throats. We will talk more about heaven in the last two chapters, but for now I want to address an area that will probably leave us the most "stunned" once we someday understand it in all its fullness. What I am referring to is how much God really does love us. Perhaps you've heard the song "I Can Only Imagine," written by Bart Millard of the group MercyMe. In the final chapter, I will share the words to this wonderful song, but for now, let me just say that we can never begin to imagine how much God loves us.

The walk of faith challenges and stretches us here on earth, but probably the greatest thing we wrestle with is trying to comprehend why and how much God loves us. Believe it or not, reliance on God's love is our chief anchor in the fight of faith. The key to faith is our *focus*. And as we saw in the last chapter, that focus is on the person of God. As we focus on God, we begin to know Him in a personal way. God welcomes this because He wants us to know Him. The Lord spoke through the prophet Jeremiah to remind us, "Let not the wise man boast of his wisdom or the strong man boast of his strength or the rich man boast of his riches, but let him who boasts boast about this: that he understands and knows me" (9:23–24). What will we discover about our God as we get to know Him? That He is a God of love, not just in a generic way but in a wonderfully specific way. God loves us. Knowing God loves us develops trust and confidence. No matter what happens to us, we can be assured that God loves us uniquely and powerfully.

An Unmistakable Statement of Love and Acceptance

If you have not camped out in Romans 8 lately, you ought to do so. Great reassurances of God's love for us reside there. The enemy of our souls would have us believe that God is displeased with us and that He has abandoned His love for us. Nothing could be further from the truth. Listen to Romans 8:31–32: "What, then, shall we say in response to this? If God is for us, who can be against us? He who did not spare his own Son, but gave him up for us all—how will he not also, along with him, graciously give us all things?"

If we stop and think about it, when we are struggling in our trials and the walk of faith becomes difficult, doesn't the love of God begin to come into question, especially God's love for us? It is not so much God's power or goodness that we question, but it is His direct care, concern, and love for *us* that we begin to question. I believe that Satan focuses much on assaulting our hearts and minds with doubts about God's love for us.

God knew we would struggle with the incredible truth that He really does love us with an intensity that is beyond imagination. That is why His love is emphasized so often in the Word. It was a passion of Paul's to get the early believers to grasp God's love for them:

> *I pray that out of his glorious riches he may strengthen you with power through his Spirit in your inner being, so that Christ may dwell in your hearts through faith. And I pray that you, being rooted and established in love, may have power, together with all the saints, to grasp how wide and long and high and deep is the love of Christ, and to know this love that surpasses knowledge—that you may be filled to the measure of all the fullness of God.* (Ephesians 3:16–19)

As my friend Doug Daily says, "Whoa baby!" What a thought—to strive to know the unknowable. The old hymn *The Love of God* puts it this way: "Could we with ink the ocean fill and were the skies of parchment made, were every stalk on earth a quill and every man a scribe by trade, to write the love of God above would drain the oceans dry, nor could the scroll contain the whole though stretched from sky to sky."

God Is Love, But Does He Love Me?

For many of us, we do believe that God is a God of love and that He has gone to great lengths to prove that. The problem is, however, that we do not believe such a love is personal and intentional. "Does God really love *me* that much?" Perhaps we view God's love as if He were standing on a great seashore and casting His net out into the sea. As He pulls in the net, all sorts of fish are flopping in there. We happen to be one of them! We view God's love as large and generic, but that is not a picture of His love. We must be convinced of His love for us if we are ever to live the life of faith marked out for us. We may not know much, and we may not always understand His ways, but we can know His heart. Let the Spirit of God encourage you with these words from Scripture:

- *The Father himself loves you.* (John 16:27)
- *But because of his great love for us, God, who is rich in mercy, made us alive with Christ even when we were dead in transgressions—it is by grace you have been saved.* (Ephesians 2:4–5)
- *[He] loves us and has freed us from our sins by his blood.* (Revelation 1:6)
- *May our Lord Jesus Christ himself and God our Father, who loved us and by his grace gave us eternal encouragement and good hope, encourage your hearts and strengthen you in every good deed and word.* (2 Thessalonians 2:16–17)

I could easily go on since the Bible has over five hundred verses that speak of the love of God. How many times does God have to tell us? And more than merely telling us, He showed us His love with the ultimate sacrifice: "Greater love has no one than this, that he lay down his life for his friends" (John 15:13). He was speaking, of course, about the Cross. Christ loves us so much that He died for us, and He died for us when we were at our worst. "You see, at just the right time, when we were still powerless, Christ died for the *ungodly.* Very rarely will anyone die for a righteous man, though for a good man someone might possibly dare to die. But God demonstrates his own love for us in this: While we were still sinners, Christ died for us" (Romans 5:6–8).

The word for *ungodly* is one of the strongest words the New Testament uses for wicked. If Satan accuses us of failing God and tells us that now God doesn't love us, remember that God has already loved us at our worst. Walter Wangerin writes, "The love of Jesus is utterly unaccountable—except that he is God, and God is love. It has no cause in us. It reacts to, or repays, or rewards just nothing in us. It is beyond human measure, beyond human comprehension. It takes my breath away."[1]

The Rock of His Love

If we know our God, then we will know that He loves us. And if we know that He loves us, our faith will remain rock solid, because it is fastened to the Rock. That means that when we are facing situations that make no sense, or when we are in the midst of some frightening times, we can still trust Him, because we are confident that He loves us. King David was a man who loved God and who understood that God loved him. He could pray confidently, "Turn, O LORD, and deliver me; save me because of your unfailing love" (Psalm 6:4).

An incident early in David's life before he was king demonstrates his confidence in God's love. In 1 Samuel 29 and 30, David and his men had set up camp at a place called Ziklag. While he and his men were gone, a band of Amalekites raided the camp, burning it to the ground and carrying away all of the women and children. When David and his men discovered this, they were very distraught and wept loudly. David's men turned their anger toward David, even though he had lost his wives as well. The situation became ugly when his men talked about stoning him.

Scripture says, "David was greatly distressed because the men were talking of stoning him; each one was bitter in spirit because of his sons and daughters. But David found strength in the LORD his God" (1 Samuel 30:6). I hope you didn't miss that important last phrase in the verse. David found strength in the Lord his God; for although all else around him was falling apart, his family was in harm's way, and those closest to him had turned against him, he still trusted his God. This is amazing! Where was the crying out against God? Why was his confidence not shaken? Because he knew his God. Perhaps that is part of the reason that God called David a man after His own heart. David may have had other problems, and he did, but he shone in the area of understanding and trusting God.

I believe the following verse can apply to what I am talking about. It is found in the book of Song of Songs, where Solomon says, "Many waters cannot quench love; rivers cannot wash it away" (8:7). If we understand the steadfast love of God, we will know that the rivers of trials that run into our lives cannot quench the love God has for us.

Years ago my parents gave me a Bible with these verses written in the front: "Fear not, for I have redeemed you; I have summoned you by name; you are mine. When you pass through the waters, I will be with you; and when you pass through the rivers, they will not sweep over you" (Isaiah 43:1–2). God's love will be the rock on which we find higher ground.

The music of Billy and Sarah Gaines has ministered to me greatly. One of Billy's songs from the album *Come On Back* is called "Other Side of This Trial."

I stand at a river; I must reach the other side.
Don't know how I will get there—the river is cold and deep and wide.
So strong is the current, I'd be surely swept away.
Stronger though is my Father's hand, and He will make a way.
This trial is that river, but I have been here before.
I've learned from the last time that I will reach the other shore.

On the other side of this trial I'll be a better man.
I will know the sweet deliverance of my Father's mighty hand.
I will have another battle won, upon which I can stand.
I'll grow closer to my Savior, as I trust His Master Plan.
I'll know Him better. I will be better. I'll be a better man.

I cried with my whole heart, "My God, what have I done
To deserve what I am going through?" He said,
"It is just that you are My son.
I'm doing a work in you, building patience in My child.

You will find on the other side, that it all has been worth the while.
So hold on to My promises as you watch My will unfold.
You'll see that this trial was under My control."

I love and want to live the words "I'll grow closer to my Savior as I trust His Master Plan." Trust will come about as we realize the unbelievable love God has for us. The psalmist was overwhelmed by it, saying, "O LORD, you have searched me and you know me. You know when I sit and when I rise; you perceive my thoughts from afar. You discern my going out and my lying down; you are familiar with all my ways. Before a word is on my tongue you know it completely, O LORD. You hem me in—behind and before; you have laid your hand upon me. Such knowledge is too wonderful for me, too lofty for me to attain" (Psalm 139:1–6). Imagine this! God knows all about us and loves us with a love that is unfathomable. The difficulty of our walk of faith will increase, but knowing God loves us will sustain us.

chapter seventeen

God Is Generous

"If you, then, though you are evil, know how to give good gifts to your children, how much more will your Father in heaven give good gifts to those who ask him!" (Matthew 7:11)

Have you ever known anyone really generous? I mean *really* generous? Every once in a while you hear about some billionaire who gives an extravagant amount of money to a charity or institution. But God is the world's most generous being. Several times in Scripture, generosity is linked with God; for example, "He poured out on us [His Holy Spirit] generously through Jesus Christ our Savior" (Titus 3:6), and "[He] gives generously to all without finding fault" (James 1:5). In response to man's belief that God's generosity is based upon our merit, Jesus told a parable found in Matthew 20 where workers were given the same pay regardless of when they joined the team and started working. In this parable, Jesus was also speaking of His generosity when the landowner posed the question, "Are you envious because I am generous?" (verse 15) to those complaining about others working less and getting the same reward.

Jesus was testifying to the goodness of the Giver, not the ones on the receiving end.

Webster's defines generous as "free in giving, bountiful, characterized by liberality." Do you think of God that way—as an incredibly generous God? Throughout this book, we have been looking at the challenges of living a life of faith. We have also noted that faith produces various results. We must not be mistaken on that point. In this life, there will be varied results to the life of faith. But here is the great news: In the next life, there will be abundant rewards. God has promised to reward us for our walk of faith, and He will reward us out of the abundant richness of His goodness.

God Has the Desire and the Means

His rewards will so outstrip our trials, suffering, and confusion here that we will be speechless and flabbergasted! I know that seems like an exaggeration. Will our rewards indeed be that great? Scripture gives a resounding yes: "No eye has seen, no ear has heard, no mind has conceived what God has prepared for those who love him" (1 Corinthians 2:9). That pretty much covers it all!

Think of a gift you'd like to give someone—one you know would be special to them, like a bike for a son, or a playhouse for a daughter, or a ring for a wife, or even a bass boat for a husband. If you had the means to do this, how special that gift would be! But think of a God who has unlimited resources and has unbelievable joy in giving. Philippians 4:19 states, "My God will meet all your needs according to his glorious riches in Christ Jesus." We normally focus on the first part of that verse about our needs being met, but notice the second part—"according to his glorious riches in Christ Jesus." God will reward us in measure with His riches in glory. How rich is God? He owns everything in this world and the entire universe!

- *"The silver is mine and the gold is mine," declares the LORD Almighty.* (Haggai 2:8)
- *Every animal of the forest is mine, and the cattle on a thousand hills. I know every bird in the mountains, and the creatures of the field are mine.* (Psalm 50:10–11)
- *"To whom will you compare me? Or who is my equal?" says the Holy One. Lift your eyes and look to the heavens: Who created all these? He who brings out the starry host one by one, and calls them each by name.* (Isaiah 40:25–26)
- *Many, O LORD my God, are the wonders you have done. The things you planned for us no one can recount to you; were I to speak and tell of them, they would be too many to declare.* (Psalm 40:5)

Better Than Our Earthly Fathers

Out of His great love, God has set up a system of rewards. He is looking forward to dispensing those rewards, most of which are in response to our walk of faith. Even our efforts to serve Him are a result of our trusting Him in obedience. These too will be rewarded. Every time you have trusted God, every time you have stepped out in faith, every time you have stayed the course and believed God in spite of circumstances, God was watching, and He will reward you.

The verse at the beginning of this chapter reminds us that if we as earthly parents know how to give good gifts, how much more our heavenly Father. The disciples, particularly Peter, wondered about God's rewards. In the story of the rich young ruler, Peter asks the Lord this question: "We have left everything to follow you! What then will there be for us?" (Matthew 19:27). Did Jesus rebuke him for this question? No, He answered it for Peter, and all who would follow Christ. Jesus said, "I tell you the truth, . . . no one who has left home or wife or brothers or parents or children for the sake of the kingdom of God will fail to receive many times as much in this age and, in the age to come, eternal life" (Luke 18:29–30). Matthew and

Mark's gospels include Jesus saying that His followers "will receive a hundred times as much" (Matthew 19:29; Mark 10:30). God will never "shortchange" anyone.

Earthly Results Are Not the Same As Heavenly Rewards

Right now it may seem like our faith is not being rewarded. The results may not always be favorable. In fact, they may seem to be just the opposite of anything remotely favorable. But your faith will be rewarded. Peter believed Jesus' words, and later Peter would write and remind each of us, "You will receive a rich welcome into the eternal kingdom of our Lord and Savior Jesus Christ" (2 Peter 1:11).

All who have placed their faith and trust in Jesus will go to heaven and spend eternity with Him. In addition to this, God has set up a system of rewards to honor those who have obeyed Christ and trusted Him in their walk of faith.

A person with great trust is given even more opportunities to trust God, and that continuous trust results in great rewards. Peter wrote of a "rich welcome," which is a phrase that the Greeks used to describe the welcome given Olympic winners when they returned home.[1] Can you imagine that type of welcome? God has much in store for those of us who have so faithfully trusted God in painful and confusing times.

I have been greatly encouraged by fellow believers who hope and long for heaven. John Ortberg writes, "The key is not positive thinking, but eschatological thinking" (which is thinking about the things of heaven and eternity).[2] Unfortunately, we live in an age of Christianity where thinking and talking about heaven is discouraged. It is not uncommon for ministers or singers to discredit eschatological thinking. They think that because there is work to do here thinking about heaven can be distracting. They say things like, "Christ will come back when He intends to, and we will be in heaven one day, but for now we are to be busy doing kingdom business." I appreciate their concerns for us to be serious about our callings here on earth, but I believe they miss the point. Thinking about heaven inspires us in this life. It gives us reason and hope. The old adage "you can be too heavenly minded to be of earthy good" is not biblical. In fact, the opposite is true—the more heavenly minded you are, the more earthly good you are. A quote by C. S. Lewis that has been used by many is quite relevant: "Aim at heaven and you will get earth thrown in. Aim at earth and you will get neither."[3] John MacArthur clarifies the erroneous thinking that thinking about heaven too much can be harmful. He contrasts the words *escape* and *endure:*

> We don't seek to escape this life by dreaming of heaven. But we do find we can endure this life because of the certainty of heaven. Heaven is eternal. Earth is temporal. Those who fix all their affections on the fleeting things of this world are the real escapists, because they are vainly attempting to avoid facing eternity—by hiding in the fleeting shadows of the things that are only transient.[4]

In his excellent book *Things Unseen,* Mark Buchanan also addresses the topic of escapism. He quotes J. R. R. Tolkien, a man who had to frequently defend his writings against criticism that they were pure escapism. Tolkien responded by saying that there are two kinds of escapism: the first is characterized by running away from life, and the second kind is characterized by running to something that is very important. Agreeing with Tolkien, Buchanan then says, "If heavenly-mindedness is a form of escapism, it is of the second kind: a remembrance and an expectancy—a groaning for home. A longing that sustains us no matter how dark it gets."[5] Buchanan likens this to a prisoner of war seeking to escape and return to his home. This will not go without reward, and God has attributed worth to your fiery trials. Much is in store for you.

Longing for Heaven

The book of Hebrews, particularly chapter 11, repeats the longings that were in the hearts of the patriarchs for something better, something eternal. These longings characterized their lives and gave them hope:

> *All these people were still living by faith when they died. They did not receive the things promised; they only saw them and welcomed them from a distance. And they admitted that they were aliens and strangers on earth. People who say such things show that they are looking for a country of their own. If they had been thinking of the country they had left, they would have had opportunity to return. Instead, they were longing for a better country—a heavenly one. Therefore God is not ashamed to be called their God, for he has prepared a city for them.* (Hebrews 11:13–16)

Did you catch that? They were longing for something better! Earlier in the chapter, it says about Abraham, "He was looking forward to the city with foundations, whose architect and builder is God" (verse 10). A passage that talks about both the Hebrew men of faith and us as well is Hebrews 11:39–40: "These were all commended for their faith, yet none of them received what had been promised. God had *planned something better for us* so that only together with us would they be made perfect."

Maybe you have trusted God, stepped out in faith, and suffered for that faith. Perhaps you didn't receive what you were looking for, because God had something better in mind. Something eternal. Like those pilgrims of old, we too are looking forward to a city. Remember Jesus' words? "In my Father's house are many rooms; if it were not so, I would have told you. I am going there to prepare a place for you" (John 14:2). Jesus is building us a place, but the address for our home is already there. "Our citizenship is in heaven. And we eagerly await a Savior from there, the Lord Jesus Christ" (Philippians 3:20). Go ahead; think about heaven, and think about your rewards. It is one of the greatest helps for our walk of faith.

Now Is the Opportunity to Win Your Rewards

The thing that we must always remind ourselves is that the opportunities to win heavenly rewards only take place here on earth. As painful and difficult as the walk of faith is, it is necessary before we receive the "glorious welcome" into eternity. Amy Carmichael wrote years ago, "We will have all of eternity to celebrate the victories, and only a few hours before sunset in which to win them."[6] Earlier, in chapter 2, we referred to 2 Corinthians 4:16–18. Verse 17 says, "For our light and momentary troubles are achieving for us an eternal glory that far outweighs them all." Paul was not making light of troubles. If anyone knew something about suffering and trials, it was the apostle Paul. But, he was saying that compared to what is being achieved for us in heaven, the troubles are light and momentary. The word *momentary* is taken from a Greek word that means "flowing as a river." It is passing by in the light of eternity.

In the book of Romans, Paul emphasizes this point dramatically: "I consider that our present sufferings are not worth comparing with the glory that will be revealed in us" (8:18). This is so hard to imagine right now. Mark Buchanan writes about what Paul said in 2 Corinthians 4:17, saying:

> *[Paul] says that trouble in this life actually achieves for us an eternal weight of glory. The Greek word for achieve is* katergazomai. *It means to make possible, to fashion, to work out for us.*
>
> *This is astounding news. Your outward wasting away, Paul says, and all that causes it, furthers it, worsens it—all these things are not just unfortunate by-products of life. They are not merely the unhappy accidents of biology, geography, chronology: being the wrong person in the wrong place at the wrong time. They are, rather, inseparable from our destiny. The trouble we are in is indispensable to the glory that awaits, raw material for a*

work of everlasting beauty. Earthly trouble achieves for us—katergazomai—the wonders of heaven.[7]

We started this chapter considering the generosity of God. I hope you have seen, or have been reminded, that His generosity knows no limits. He could choose to reward you right here and now on this earth and in this lifetime. Some have experienced a bit of that already. But that is nothing like what is in store for His children in eternity. And for those of you who have been stretched and tried and are still looking for your reward, be assured that it is coming, and it will be beyond what you could have ever imagined. "God is not unjust; he will not forget your work and the love you have shown him" (Hebrews 6:10). Let's spend the last chapter thinking about what those rewards might look like . . . remembering that they will still be beyond what we can come up with!

chapter eighteen

Your Reward, Beyond Imagination

You will be a crown of splendor in the LORD's hand, a royal diadem in the hand of your God. (Isaiah 62:3)

Bev and I had been planning our trip to Tahiti, Bora Bora, and Moorea for months. The brochures and magazines we looked at presented us with pictures unlike any place on earth we had visited. Not only were the islands beautiful, but the underwater scenes were phenomenal. We are both divers and could not wait to slip below the surface of the South Pacific and the island lagoons. No matter what happened in the preceding months, one glance at the calendar reminded us of our upcoming trip. It lifted our spirits and filled us with wild imagination. We read and researched as much as we could. We felt we knew the islands and were somehow experiencing them already. And then the day came when we landed by small plane in Bora Bora. Our faces were pressed against the window of the plane, trying to take in the sights as we began our descent.

During our stay we made memories that will last a lifetime

—from our boat trip, to our bungalow over the water, to the scuba diving, to strolls on the beach. The brochures and the magazines, though colorful and informative, did not begin to reveal the half of our vacation destination.

More Than the Bible Conveys

The Bible is our sourcebook for heaven and the rewards that await us there. There are wonderful pictures and descriptions about heaven revealed on the pages of Scripture. But at their best, they are somewhat cryptic and fall so far short of causing us to realize the grandeur and splendor of heaven. This is not a knock on the infallible Word of God. But heaven and the rewards awaiting us cannot be described adequately in Scripture. Heaven is too big for that—and so is God.

Our earthly knowledge of His goodness only begins to scratch the surface. Besides, our reference points and vocabulary for understanding the glories of heaven are restricted to earth. Perhaps that is why the apostle Paul said only these words after getting a firsthand view of heaven: I "was caught up to paradise . . . [I] heard inexpressible things, things that man is not permitted to tell" (2 Corinthians 12:4). One translation of this verse says Paul "heard things that can't be expressed in words, things that humans cannot put into words" (12:4 GW). If you have read the book of Revelation, you've witnessed the challenge that the apostle John had describing the end time events and particularly the glories of heaven. How can you describe the indescribable?

Heaven Is Where God Is

Let's take a look at some of John's description of our new home in heaven:

> *"Now the dwelling of God is with men, and he will live with them. They will be his people, and God himself will be with them*

> *and be their God. He will wipe away every tear from their eyes. There will be no more death or mourning or crying or pain, for the old order of things has passed away." . . . No longer will there be any curse. The throne of God and of the Lamb will be in the city, and his servants will serve him. They will see his face, and his name will be on their foreheads. There will be no more night. They will not need the light of a lamp or the light of the sun, for the Lord God will give them light. And they will reign for ever and ever.* (Revelation 21:3–4; 22:3–5)

There are many wonderful things listed in that passage, but John wants to make sure that we realize that the most important thing is that God will be there. We will be with our God! No longer any separation. Centuries before Revelation was written, the book of Psalms contained words that still echo the cries of the hearts of men and women today:

> *One thing I ask of the LORD, this is what I seek: that I may dwell in the house of the LORD all the days of my life, to gaze upon the beauty of the LORD and to seek him in his temple.* (27:4)

> *You have made known to me the path of life; you will fill me with joy in your presence, with eternal pleasures at your right hand.* (16:11)

> *As the deer pants for streams of water, so my soul pants for you, O God. My soul thirst for God, for the living God. When can I go and meet with God?* (42:1–2)

The thought of one day being with our blessed Savior can be the help and strength we need to get us through the most trying of situations.

Not All Will Receive the Same Rewards

But here is a reminder. Your rewards will not only be heaven and the presence of God, as awesome as that is. Your rewards will be tangible and specific to you. God will reward you for your life of faith. And the more you have trusted Him, the more He will reward you. Not everyone going to heaven will be rewarded equally. Some will receive far greater rewards because of the difficult life of faith they were called on to live. The Lord Jesus Christ made this clear in His parables of the minas and talents (see Luke 19 and Matthew 25). Those who have had to suffer more and those who have been called to trust more will receive more. The basis for our rewards will not be based on successes and achievements. Some of those who receive the greatest honor in heaven will be those who on earth were relatively unknown. In her book *Heaven: Your Real Home,* Joni Eareckson Tada writes, "Please note Jesus doesn't say, 'Because you've been successful in a very small matter,' He says, 'Because you've been trustworthy.' God is not scrutinizing the success of your marriage or judging the results of your ministry . . . Success isn't the key. Faithfulness is."[1]

What will those rewards look like? That is a great question, and one that is not clearly explained in Scripture. They may include the following:

1. *Special crowns.* Scripture seems to reveal at least four crowns that can be won: the incorruptible crown (1 Corinthians 9:25); the crown of righteousness (2 Timothy 4:8); the crown of glory (1 Peter 5:4); and the crown of life (James 1:12). The crown of life specifically seems to fit in with faith demonstrated during trials (Revelation 2:10).
2. *Greater responsibility in reigning with Christ.* In both the parables of the minas and the talents, Jesus rewards the faithfulness of His servants by placing them in leadership. In the parable of the minas, they are placed in charge of cities. In the parable of the talents, He simply says He will put them in charge of many things.
3. *Unusual proximity to the throne of God.* Perhaps we are most uncomfortable with this one. But heaven is a real

place, and God is serious about rewarding those who have trusted Him in the greatest of trials. Do you think a just God would call some on earth to experience more severe trials and then just give them the same rewards that others will receive? Revelation 7:14–17 seems to reveal the special place of blessing around the throne that God offers to those who have suffered much.

4. *A greater eternal dwelling place.* Jesus said He was going to prepare a place for us. Will all the rooms and the mansions look the same? I doubt it. God is a creative God. He is into beauty and extravagance. Why wouldn't God reward His children thusly? He says of them: "'They will be mine,' says the LORD Almighty, 'in the day when I make up my treasured possession'" (Malachi 3:17). I am sure that God will give each "treasured possession" of His an unbelievably beautiful dwelling. Yet perhaps God will do His best work for those who have trusted Him most. Remember Paul said that our afflictions are achieving for us an eternal glory.

As we are reaching the conclusion of this chapter and the book, I hope to encourage each of us with what is in store for us in heaven. I realize that as I attempt to describe heaven, I am looking through a dark glass and cannot see it clearly (1 Corinthians 13:12). But even this attempt has value as we are told to "set your hearts on things above, where Christ is seated at the right hand of God. Set your minds on things above, not on earthly things" (Colossians 3:1–2). Joseph Stowell encourages us with these words: "Living in the reality of heaven has tremendous relevance. When we envision heaven as our home, everything in life is radically rearranged. It affects our posture towards God, our possessions, people, pain, and pleasure. And heaven in our hearts purifies us and alters our sense of identity."[2] Here are some things to look forward to in heaven:

Heaven is the place where God is. We will be with our God forever. The greatest thing about heaven is that our God lives and reigns there. We will regularly see our blessed Savior.

Heaven is the place where worship is unhindered. We were made for worship, and God desires worship. It will be our joyful experience throughout eternity to worship Him. The flesh, restraints of time, and personal agendas will all be done away with. We will get the opportunity to drown out the anthem of the angels!

Heaven is the place where we will be done with sin in the body. Can you even imagine that? Sin has so defined, shaped, and hindered us that we cannot imagine what total freedom from it will be like. We will never struggle with sin again.

Heaven is the place where we will walk by sight and not by faith. What will that be like? We have always been called upon to walk by faith. When we are in heaven we will realize that this life on earth was the only opportunity we had to walk by faith.

Heaven is the place where we will enjoy new bodies. If you are young and healthy, you probably cannot appreciate this fact of heaven as much. But we will finally put off this temporal body that is so subject to wear and tear. We will have a glorious body like our blessed Savior. No restrictions, no limitations. (Maybe I'll be able to dunk a basketball again!)

Heaven is the place of incredible fun and happiness. We will not be bored in heaven. No way! God designed pleasures, and no one throws a party like God. There will be the best food and drink, and we won't have to worry about calories and sickness.

Heaven is the place of ultimate consolation. Oh, the pain that fills this earth right now. God will somehow make it better. He will not only wipe away every tear, but He will personally console each individual who needs it.

Heaven is the place where we'll reunite with loved ones. There is no sorrow like the separation of loved ones. All those who have gone before will be reunited with us—husbands and wives, sons and daughters, mothers and fathers, all of our loved ones and friends, never to be separated again.

Heaven is the place where relationships deepen. Most of us have heard stories of heaven being the place where we will be like the angels. We won't have relationships, marriages will not be in existence anymore, and we will all be one big happy family. Well, heaven is a place of more, not less. We won't walk by our loved ones and say a casual hello. God ordained the family, and it will be at its greatest in heaven. I'm looking forward to spending eternity with my family.

Heaven is the place where we'll meet those we have prayed for. What a great day it will be to finally meet those whom we have prayed for. And not only to meet those we have prayed for, but those who have prayed for us. Maybe this is a time when God wipes away all tears, for this seems like when they would be shed. Heaven will also be the place to meet those who have benefited from our missionary giving and to meet those who have given sacrificially for us.

Heaven is the place of incredible beauty. Look at God's great work in creating the heavens and the earth. Can you imagine what heaven will look like? It will be more than streets of gold and gates of pearl. God is into mountains, trees, rivers, meadows, and flowers. Our senses will come alive enjoying His creation.

Heaven is the place of endless exploration. Why did God create an infinite universe? Why all the stars and planets? Is it for us to enjoy too? Will part of God's design for eternity be unlimited exploration? I believe so.

Heaven is the place where we'll enjoy God's vast creative skills. Think of how creative God is. Look at the animal world—the mammals, reptiles, fish, and birds. The colors, shapes, and sounds of each animal. Can you imagine what heaven must be like? What new creatures will we see? Will we have our own pets? (Our daughter Jessica is convinced God will reassemble our dog Clancy's DNA and have him in heaven.) Will you have your own winged horse to fly?

Heaven is the place where our knowledge will expand. I don't know if it is true that we use only 10 percent of our brains. But God has given us minds that will be able to grasp eternity. We will learn and grow—never will things become boring and stale. We will have all of eternity to learn about God.

Heaven is the place of joyful service. We were built for worship and service. God will allow His servants to joyfully serve Him throughout eternity. What we have done down here, in this brief amount of time, is the rehearsal for eternity. We will never be bored, and we will be thrilled to serve God forever.

We Will Hear God Say, "Well-Done, Well-Done Indeed."

We have taken a long journey of faith in this book. Somehow, now, just talking about heaven puts it all into proper perspective. And that is what will happen one day when we step on heaven's golden shore. It will be worth it all.

Earlier in this book, I mentioned to you my enjoyment of hiking Pike's Peak, the 14,110-foot mountain near my house. I will never forget the first time I hiked to the top. On the way up, a large group of college students from a local church passed me. We chatted briefly as we walked along, sharing our common faith together.

Hours later, as I was rounding a bend, I saw the finish line. Standing on either side of the finish line was this large group of students. As I approached the end of the hike, they broke out in cheers—for me! Several left their places on the sides of the trail and came down to congratulate me. They slapped me on the back and repeatedly said, "Well-done, well-done indeed." I will never forget that moment. After the grueling, exhausting climb to the top, they were waiting for me at the finish line to congratulate me and tell me that the journey was well done. I don't know who in the group came up with that biblical idea to encourage me, but may the Lord bless him mightily.

That day, in a very real way, I had a picture and a reminder of what that final day will be like. One day, not only the host of heaven will congratulate us, but our blessed Savior will step forward and say, "Well done, good and faithful servant! You have been faithful with a few things; I will put you in charge of many things. Come and share your master's happiness!" (Matthew 25:21). What will my response be? What will I do or say?

I can only imagine what it will be like,
When I walk by Your side.
I can only imagine what my eyes will see,
When Your face is before me.
I can only imagine.

Surrounded by Your glory,
What will my heart feel?
Will I dance for You, Jesus?

Or in awe of You be still?
Will I stand in Your presence
Or to my knees will I fall?
Will I sing hallelujah?
Will I be able to speak at all?
I can only imagine.
I can only imagine.

I can only imagine when that day comes,
And I find myself standing in the Son.
I can only imagine when all I will do,
Is forever, forever worship You.
I can only imagine.
I can only imagine.

—MercyMe, "I Can Only Imagine,"
from the album *Almost There*

Notes

CHAPTER 1: WHERE IS GOD?

1. C. S. Lewis, *A Grief Observed* (New York: Bantam, 1976), 4–5.
2. Erwin W. Lutzer, *Why Good People Do Bad Things* (Nashville: Word, 2001), 114.

CHAPTER 2: WHAT IS FAITH?

1. Kristen Stagg, *If God Should Choose* (Chicago: Moody, 2002), 204.
2. James William Baird, *Thunder Over Scotland* (Campbell, Calif.: Green Leaf, 1982), 186–87.
3. W. Ian Thomas, *The Mystery of Godliness* (Grand Rapids: Zondervan, 1972), 35.
4. J. C. Pollock, *Hudson Taylor and Maria: Pioneers in Christ* (New York: McGraw-Hill, 1962), 197.

CHAPTER 3: MORE VALUABLE THAN GOLD

1. Gerald Sittser, *A Grace Disguised* (Grand Rapids: Zondervan, 1996), 143.

2. David Jeremiah, *My Heart's Desire: Living Every Moment in the Wonder of Worship* (Nashville: Integrity, 2002), 165–66.

Chapter 5: Going Down with God

1. Rick Warren, *The Purpose Driven Life: What on Earth Am I Here For?* (Grand Rapids: Zondervan, 2002), 49–50.

Chapter 7: Knowing the Game Plan

1. C. H. MacIntosh, *The MacIntosh Treasury* (Neptune, N.J.: Loizeaux Brothers, 1978), 482.

Chapter 8: Armed for Conflict

1. Arthur Bennett, ed., *The Valley of Vision* (Pennsylvania: Banner of Truth Trust, 2001), 181.

Chapter 9: Trials, a Necessary Process

1. Amy Carmichael as quoted by J. Oswald Sanders, *Spiritual Leadership: Principles of Excellence for Every Believer* (Chicago: Moody, 1994), 116–17.

Chapter 12: What Should I Expect?

1. Jim Cymbala, *Fresh Faith: What Happens When Real Faith Ignites God's People* (Grand Rapids: Zondervan, 1999), 97.
2. Ibid., 102.
3. Dave Dravecky, *Do Not Lose Heart* (Grand Rapids: Zondervan, 1998), 30.

Chapter 13: Faith's Affirmation

1. J. Oswald Sanders, *Bible Men of Faith* (Chicago: Moody, 1974), 9.

Chapter 16: Rock Solid About God's Love

1. Walter Wangerin Jr., *Reliving the Passion* (Grand Rapids: Zondervan, 1992), 54.

Chapter 17: God Is Generous

1. Warren Wiersbe, *The Bible Exposition Commentary* (Wheaton: Victor, 1989), 440.
2. John Ortberg, *The Life You've Always Wanted* (Grand Rapids: Zondervan, 2002), 73.

3. C. S. Lewis, *Mere Christianity* (New York: Macmillan, 1960), 118.
4. John MacArthur, *The Glory of Heaven* (Wheaton: Crossway, 1996), 51.
5. Mark Buchanan, *Things Unseen: Living in Light of Forever* (Sisters, Oreg.: Multnomah, 2002), 22.
6. Amy Carmichael as quoted by Joni Eareckson Tada, *Heaven: Your Real Home* (Grand Rapids: Zondervan, 1995), 195.
7. Buchanan, *Things Unseen,* 185.

Chapter 18: Your Reward, Beyond Imagination

1. Tada, *Heaven,* 67.
2. Joseph M. Stowell, *Eternity: Reclaiming a Passion for What Endures* (Chicago: Moody, 1995), 110.

SINCE 1894, Moody Publishers has been dedicated to equip and motivate people to advance the cause of Christ by publishing evangelical Christian literature and other media for all ages, around the world. Because we are a ministry of the Moody Bible Institute of Chicago, a portion of the proceeds from the sale of this book go to train the next generation of Christian leaders.

If we may serve you in any way in your spiritual journey toward understanding Christ and the Christian life, please contact us at www.moodypublishers.com.

"All Scripture is God-breathed and is useful for teaching, rebuking, correcting and training in righteousness, so that the man of God may be thoroughly equipped for every good work."

—2 TIMOTHY 3:16, 17

THE NAME YOU CAN TRUST®

The Fight of Faith Team

Acquiring Editor
Greg Thornton

Copy Editor
Ali Childers

Back Cover Copy
Anne Perdicaris

Cover Design
Paetzold Associates

Cover Photo
Comstock Images/Getty Images

Interior Design
Ragont Design

Printing and Binding
Versa Press, Inc.

The typeface for the text of this book is Fairffield LH